Just Enough
to Make a Story

A Sourcebook for
Storytelling

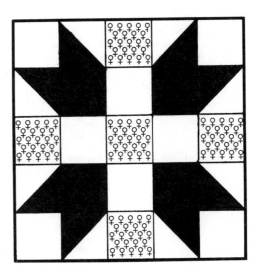

BY NANCY SCHIMMEL

SISTERS'
CHOICE
PRESS

SECOND
EDITION
1982

Copyright © 1978, 1982 by Nancy Schimmel
Published in the United States by Sisters' Choice Press, 2027 Parker Street,
Berkeley, CA 94704. Single and bulk copies available by mail.
Second edition, 1982.

Quotation on page 36 from *The Lives of Children* by George Dennison.
Copyright © 1970, Random House, Inc. Used with the permission of
Random House, Inc.

Quotation on page 37 from *The Joys of Yiddish* by Leo Rosten. Copyright
© 1968, McGraw-Hill Book Company. Used with the permission of
McGraw-Hill Book Company.

"Barney McCabe" from *Ain't You Got a Right to the Tree of Life* by Guy Carawan
and Candie Carawan. Copyright © 1966 by Guy and Candie Carawan.
Used with the permission of Guy Carawan.

Cataloging in publication data:

Schimmel, Nancy
    Just enough to make a story: A sourcebook for storytellers, by Nancy
Schimmel. Revised edition.
    1. Storytelling   2. Women in folklore and mythology—Bibliography
    3. Fairy tales—Bibliography   I. Title
LB1042.S35   372.2'14
ISBN 0-932164-02-1

Book design by Nancy Schimmel with lotsa help
Typeset by *turnaround*, Berkeley and San Francisco, in Palatino
Layout by Graphic Eye
Printed by Up Press, Palo Alto

ACKNOWLEDGMENTS

I would like to thank

my students, who taught me much that is in this book and with whom I worked out how to say it all

all the storytellers, particularly Connie Regan and Barbara Freeman, whose FOLKTELLERS was a model for SISTERS' CHOICE

Elizabeth Sor, who taught me the paperfolds I used in "The Handsome Prince" and worked out the instructions for them

Tom Riles, who photographed me flying a goose girl at
A Room of One's Own

all the anonymous quiltmakers, mostly women, whose artistry and imagination provided this work with illustrations and SISTERS' CHOICE with a name and logo

Ruth Burnstein, who drew the music

Carolyn Rabun and Claudia Morrow, who found the mistakes

Carole Leita, who read, reread, organized, criticized, proofed, indexed, and blew bubbles

Gay Ducey and Kitty Farrell, who helped make the second edition new

for my parents, who told me their stories

for Carole, who listens to mine

Table of Contents

INTRODUCTION TO THE SECOND EDITION

THE FOUR YEARS since this book was written have been years of tremendous growth in storytelling—word of the renaissance has even reached *Time* (August 13, 1981, p. 6+) and *Newsweek* (November 9, 1981, p. 84). Festivals and resources—recorded, videotaped, filmed and live—have multiplied. Interest in storytelling to older adults has increased. And, as part of Catherine Horne Farrell's Word Weaving project in San Francisco Bay Area schools, I have begun to seek out research in the effects of storytelling on learning. All these changes had to be reflected in *Just Enough to Make a Story*.

In the second and third printings I had updated resource lists and corrected the errors and out-of-date addresses of the first printing, but the changes this time seem to warrant calling this a new edition. I have added a tandem version of "The Pancake," and a list of stories suggested for telling or reading to adults, including some stories that work with junior-high audiences.

As I prepare this edition I am also completing an album called *Plum Pudding: Stories and Songs with Nancy Schimmel and the Plum City Players*. It is intended for children age eight and up, and for adults, and will be available from Sisters' Choice. I tell "The Tailor" from this book, "Umai" from Theodora Kroeber's *The Inland Whale,* and a story I wrote called "The Woodcutter's Story." Bonnie Lockhart sings her "Witch Song," I sing my song about Annie Oakley, "Little Sure Shot," Amunka Dávila sings a traditional Latin American song, "Al Tambor," and we all sing "A Place in the Choir."

Next comes a book of stories and songs, including the ones on *Plum Pudding*. It will be called *A Second Helping* and should be out in 1983.

NOTE

Stories mentioned in the text without source are listed with source in "Sisters' Choices" at the end of the book.

Introduction : The Tailor

IN A VILLAGE ONCE lived a poor tailor. He had made overcoats for many people, but he had never made one for himself, though an overcoat was the one thing he wanted. He never had enough money to buy material and set it aside for himself, without making something to sell. But he saved and saved, bit by bit, and at last he had saved enough.

He bought the cloth and cut it carefully, so as not to waste any. He sewed up the coat, and it fit him perfectly. He was proud of that coat. He wore it even when it was the least bit cold. He wore it until it was all worn out.

At least he thought it was worn out, but then he looked closely and he could see that there was just enough good material left to make a jacket. So he cut up the coat and made a jacket. It fit just as well as the coat, and he could wear it even more often. He wore it until it was all worn out.

At least it seemed to be all worn out, but he looked again, and he could see that there was still enough good material to make a vest. So he cut up the jacket and sewed up a vest. He tried it on, and he looked most distinguished. He wore that vest every single day. He wore it until it was all worn out.

At least he thought it was all worn out, but when he looked it over carefully, he saw some places here and there that were not worn. So he cut them out, sewed them together, and made a cap. He tried it on, and it looked just right. He wore it outdoors and in, until it was all worn out.

At least it seemed to be all worn out, but when he looked, he could see that there was just enough left to make a button. So he cut up the cap and made a button. It was a good button. He wore it every day, until it was all worn out.

At least he thought it was all worn out, but when he looked closely, he could see that there was just enough left of that button to make a story, so he made a story out of it and I just told it to you.

Now I didn't make a story out of a button, but I did make it out of a song. A long time ago, I heard someone sing a Yiddish folk song at a concert and explain in English what the song said, which was the same as the story except that the person in the song made a song instead of a story out of the button.* I didn't remember the song, but I liked the idea, and years later I tried it out as a story.

I was working at a library that was just a block from a convalescent hospital. I told stories once a month at the hospital, and each time, after I did my stories and songs, we would sit around at tables and have tea and cookies. About the third time I went there, I told "The Tailor." Afterwards, I sat at a table with a man and a woman. The woman said, "You know, it's funny you told the story about a tailor today, because my father was a tailor. He was in Germany and he wanted to come to this country but he didn't have enough money, so he stowed away. When the ship had gotten out to sea, he poked his nose out of his hiding place and went out to see if it was safe. He overheard someone saying they were looking for a tailor, so he went right back to his hiding place and stayed there. At the end of the trip, he found out that they were just looking for a tailor to do some tailoring, they weren't looking for a stowaway at all, and he had missed out on a job."

I said, "That's funny that you're telling me this story about your father who was a tailor, because my grandfather was a tailor. His family scraped up enough money to send him to this country, but he didn't like it. He had been a tailor's apprentice in Budapest, but in New York he was working in a sweatshop, and the streets weren't paved with gold after all, and he was homesick. He was living with his uncle, but it wasn't home. On the Sabbath, on Saturdays, he would go down to the docks and look wistfully at the ships and think about Budapest. One day a man who spoke Yiddish came up to him and asked why he looked so sad. He said he was

---

*The song, in English, is available on *Songs of the Holidays* sung by Gene Bluestein on Folkways FC 7554. It is called "I Had a Little Coat."

wishing he could go home on one of these ships, but he didn't have the money. The man said, 'Well, I can take care of you. You just sign on as part of the crew, and work your way across. When you get where you want to go, you jump ship and you're home.' My grandfather thought that was a fine idea, and he signed his name here, and he signed his name there, and he was in the U.S. Navy for four years.

"Luckily, he liked the Navy, and he re-enlisted twice, and at the end of his service he became a naval tailor, which he was until the day he died. And since he was on a ship with a crew of New York Irish, this Jewish tailor from Budapest spoke English with a bit of an Irish brogue until he day he died."

After the woman and I had this little exchange, the man, who had been just sitting there not saying a word, said "What did you say the tailor made out of the button?"

"A story."

He said, "What?"

I said, "A story. Out of the button he made the story I told you."

"Oh!" he said, "I thought you said *buttonhole*."

The man had a pretty good story there. Not the story I told, but one that makes sense, because after the button wears out you've got nothing left, and what do you make out of nothing? You make a hole. And what kind of a hole does a tailor make? A buttonhole.

And indeed this is the way stories and songs change. A word goes through a change of time or place, or through a hearing aid, and comes out nonsense. The listener, who becomes the next teller, changes the word so it makes sense again.

We all have stories: stories that are handed down in our families, stories and jokes that we hear and retell with small changes, and stories about things that happen to us, like the story I just told about the time I went to the convalescent hospital in Belmont. Some of us are professional storytellers, some of us are amateurs, some tell out of choice and some out of necessity, but we are all storytellers, even if the only stories we tell are stories about why we were late to work this morning.

We are all storytellers, but some of us tell stories better, some of us tell better stories, and some of us are better at remembering the right story for the right moment. The skills of choosing, learning and telling stories can be acquired, and I have tried to pass on some of what I know about them in this book. I believe one can also acquire the attitudes that help a storyteller. By reading about folklore and by reading and hearing and telling many tales, one learns to respect the story, making it one's own without wrenching it from its tradition, or meaning, or changing a special flavor it might have. By choosing well and telling stories over and over, one gains enough confidence in the story so that one does not need to dress it up with unnecessary dramatics or props. "Unnecessary" is, of course, a matter of taste, but props should be props, not crutches. And as one learns the stories well, one can pay more attention to the audience, and change the telling or choice of story in response to its mood. I am still learning to tell stories I have told for years, and still learning to sound like myself as I tell them.

I have included stories in this book, as well as ideas on how to tell them. It is with some reluctance that I put down on paper the stories I have been telling. They change every time I tell them, every time anyone tells them. But sometimes people can't remember even enough to tell at all, and they ask me, "Is this story written down?" Until now, I have had to answer "No," or "Yes, but it's out of print." So here they are, locked inside this book. It is up to you to release them.

Choosing a Story

AT THE END OF A STORYTELLING COURSE, one of my students said, "I was disappointed at first that you didn't just tell us how to tell stories; then I realized that you couldn't." And indeed I cannot. I can give some ideas, but people tell stories successfully so many ways that I can't find any hard and fast rules. Except maybe one, which is, tell stories you like to tell. And that rule has two sides to it. One is enjoying the story itself for whatever reason—the plot, the language, the associations it has for you. The other is enjoying the telling, which depends somewhat on the effect the story has on the audience—an effect you can't always predict when you choose the story. I can tell you how *I* find, learn, and tell stories, and what works for other storytellers I know. You can pick out what works for you.

I have to read, and hear, and sift through many stories to find one I want to make the effort to learn and tell. When I hear a story told, even badly told, I can judge it better than when I read it. If I read a story I think I like well enough, I read it aloud to myself, a friend or a tape recorder, usually all three, before I decide.

A good story to tell can have complex language but it should have a fairly simple plot, without sub-plots and digressions—unless digressions are the point of the story, as in Mark Twain's "The Notorious Jumping Frog of Calaveras County." The main action should begin fairly quickly, without too much intro-duction. It helps if the plot comes to a satisfying conclusion, so the listeners know the story is over. A formula ending, like "Snip, snap, snout, this tale's told out," can serve the same purpose. If I am telling a story from my own experience, I try to apply some of the same criteria—sorting out the important from the unimportant details, making sure the introduction (why I was where it happened, who the other characters were) doesn't outweigh the story itself.

If I like the point or the plot of a story but not the telling, I look for another version before I decide to cut or change the story myself. For instance, I liked the plot of "The Peddler of Ballaghadereen" (*Way of the Storyteller*), and the language was fine, but the introduction seemed too long for the message about belief in dreams that drew me to the story. So I

went to "The Pedlar of Swaffham" (*More English Fairy Tales*), and found a briefer telling in which the message had relatively more importance. If you do want to cut a story, both Colwell and DeWit (listed at the end of this chapter) discuss how to do it. In some stories, it is the language itself, and the mood it sets, that I feel are the most important, not the plot. Learning these stories word for word is more difficult for me than learning a plot and telling it in my own words, but it is very satisfying.

Language can help make a story easier to learn. Verse is easier to memorize than prose, and recurring rhymes or rhythmic phrases in a story give both teller and listener something familiar to hang on to. Most stories in easy-to-learn forms—cumulative tales like "The Old Woman and Her Pig," stories with repetition of rhymes and phrases like "The Three Billy Goats Gruff"—are nursery tales best told to children under eight. But there are some that can be told to older children and adults. "The Tailor" is one that works for all ages, "Lazy Jack" for older as well as younger children, "The Yellow Ribbon" (*Juba This and Juba That*) for older children. "Mr. Fox" is an easy-to-learn story that I tell to adults rather than to children.

If the language of a story does not make it easy to learn, a very logical, sequential plot may help. In "The Little Red Hen," for instance, the wheat must be planted before it is cut, threshed before it is milled, and so on, whereas the mishaps that befall "The Husband Who Was to Mind the House" (*Womenfolk and Fairy Tales*) could conceivably happen in some other sequence than they do, so they don't order themselves in the memory without some effort.

A shorter story is usually easier to learn, but not always. "The King o' the Cats" is about half as long as "Lazy Jack," but I found it more difficult to learn and tell, because it is a story within a story, and I found I had to stick closer to the exact wording or get mixed up.

A teller is sometimes requested to tell a story from a particular culture or one pointing a particular moral, and can't find one that he or she likes well enough to learn. Before I learn a story I feel lukewarm about, I try to find a substitute—a poem, a song, a picture book, a well-written non-fiction book from which I can read aloud or tell, even a craft I can demonstrate. For instance, *The Last Free Bird* by A. Harris Stone (Prentice-Hall, 1967) is a picture book on ecology that can be used with all ages above pre-school; *They Put on Masks* by Byrd Baylor (Scribner, 1974) is beautifully written and illustrated non-fiction on the use of masks in Native American ceremonials. This may also be a time to read a story aloud instead of learning it. Even reading aloud takes some preparation—a practice out loud for smoothness and emphasis; taping and listening, if possible, for clarity—but it doesn't take the devotion that learning does.

While it's a good idea to tell only stories you like, it is possible to find a *kind* of story you like and feel safe with, and not try other kinds—to tell only funny stories, or fairy tales, or whatever your preference is. Not that you should feel bad about neglecting a kind you don't like after you've given it a fair try; the closest I can get to telling a fable is to tell one of James Thurber's *Fables for Our Time* (Harper, 1940), and I only learned that at the request of a teacher who was doing a unit on fables. But you never know—a little experimenting, even under duress, may open to you a whole body of stories you never thought you could tell.

You may read dozens of stories for each one you learn. It's a good idea to list these somewhere—copying title pages from story collections and making notes on them is an easy way—so that later, when someone asks you for a story about guinea pigs, or whatever, you won't go crazy trying to remember where you saw one.

More of the stories I tell come from Joseph Jacobs' two volumes of *English Folk and Fairy Tales* than from any other single source. Many tellers I know also find these stories easy and satisfying to learn and tell, but others will have their own favorites. My second source of stories is the oral tradition itself, stories I have heard but not found in books. Many of the stories I tell can now be found in *Womenfolk and Fairy Tales*. Following this chapter I've listed some books that contain good stories to start on. The children's librarian at your nearest library can help you find others, and you can find them yourself if the library has any of these guides:

Folklore of the North American Indians: An Annotated Bibliography. Compiled by Judith C. Ullom. Library of Congress, 1969.

Index to Fairy Tales, Myths and Legends. Basic volume and two supplements edited by Mary Huse Eastman, third supplement edited by Norma O. Ireland. Faxon, 1926–1973. Not selective, but the third supplement is useful for finding stories by subject.

Stories: A List of Stories to Tell and to Read Aloud. New York Public Library. 7th edition, 1977.

Stories to Tell: A List of Stories with Annotations. Jeanne Hardendorff, comp. Enoch Pratt Free Library, Baltimore. 5th edition, 1965.

Storyteller's Sourcebook . . . A Subject, Title, and Motif Index to Folklore Collections for Children. Margaret Read MacDonald, ed. Gale, 1982. Annotated index to stories in collections listed in *Children's Catalog* from 1961 to 1981.

STORY COLLECTIONS

Arbuthnot, May Hill. *The Arbuthnot Anthology of Children's Literature.* Scott, Foresman, 1976.

Courlander, Harold. *The Hat-Shaking Dance and Other Ashanti Tales from Ghana.* Harcourt, 1957 (plus his other collections from Africa, Asia, Haiti and North America).

Ginsburg, Mirra. *Three Holes and One Doughnut: Fables from Russia.* Dial, 1970.

Jacobs, Joseph. *English Folk and Fairy Tales.* Putnam, 1904, Dover reprint as *English Fairy Tales* (plus his other collections from the British Isles).

Minard, Rosemary. *Womenfolk and Fairy Tales.* Houghton, 1975.

Phelps, Ethel Johnston. *Tatterhood and Other Tales.* Feminist Press, 1978.

Rockwell, Anne. *The Three Bears and 15 Other Stories.* Crowell, 1975.

Ross, Eulalie Steinmetz. *The Lost Half-Hour, A Collection of Stories.* Harcourt, 1963.

Tashjian, Virginia. *Juba This and Juba That: Story Hour Stretches for Large and Small Groups.* Little, 1969. *With a Deep Sea Smile: Story Hour Stretches.* Little, 1974.

Withers, Carl. *World of Nonsense.* Holt, 1968, o.p. (and his other collections).

Learning a Story

THE ONLY RULE I KNOW for learning a story is: learn the plot first, then learn the words if you want to. If you learn the words only, and forget one, you might get stuck; but if you know the sequence of events, and forget a word, you can fake it till you pick up the thread of the words again.

People have different methods of learning plots. Some visualize the events, scenes, characters; running this movie over inside their heads until the sequence is fixed; then describing it out loud in their own words or learning the subtitles already written by the author or reteller. I can't do this, so I learn by logic—trying to reconstruct the sequence in my mind, realizing that this incident can't happen until that one has. This way I get the events organized; then I try to do the same thing aloud. I must use words to think through the plot, and I may then have to unlearn them if I decide to use the author's, or reteller's, words, so visualizing is probably the better method for those who can do it.

I find learning the plot the most difficult and least enjoyable part of being a storyteller. A beginner may want to start with a story already pretty familiar, either a favorite from one's own childhood or a book one has read aloud many times. I had read *Caps for Sale* over and over at library story-times, but didn't know I could tell it without the book until I was telling stories at a neighborbood art fair and didn't have the book with me. I tried it anyway, and surprised myself. I have never used the book since.

Once I have learned the plot, I usually read the story aloud several times, or listen to it on the tape recorder (a good method to use while driving). Then I usually memorize the first paragraph or two (as insurance against stage fright), any rhymed or repeated phrases, and probably the ending, especially if it is a formula ending. By this time I am familiar enough with the words to know whether I like them so well that I want to memorize them all, whether I prefer the words I found in learning the plot, or whether I want to try for something in between—getting closer to the written words without memorizing, which means more checking back to the original as I work, but not working from it.

As to whether memorizing or telling in one's own words is more traditional, that depends on the tradition. An Inuit storyteller is corrected if the story is not told exactly the same each time, while Zunis prefer a teller who embroiders on the basic plot. In the Anglo-American tradition, the tale tends to be a free-phrase form, meaning that the words are subject to change, in contrast to proverbs and charms, which are fixed-phrase. If a riddle or proverb appears in a story, it will not change much, even though the rest of the story is retold in entirely different words. Ballads and other stories told in rhyme are fixed-phrase throughout. While they are easier to memorize, there is much less freedom, within the rhyme and rhythm, to fake it if you forget a word or two.

Usually I decide to use the author's words if the story is not a folktale, or if the tale is retold so well that any change seems to weaken it. Sometimes, however, the plot itself hinges on the exact wording of the dialogue, as in "Clever Manka" or "Ticoumba and the President." Then the dialogue at least must be memorized. I also try to remember turns of phrase that seem to characterize a region or culture or a particular story. However, I don't try to reproduce a regional dialect throughout a story. In "Barney McCabe," for instance, I keep "That ain't nothing but your grandma frock-tail switchin' to get your supper hot," but I substitute "master" for "maussa"

and "we're very tired" for "we very tired." Unless a teller has lived in the region, it is difficult, if not impossible, to reproduce dialect naturally and correctly, without overdoing it. It is impossible to do so from the written word, as you can tell by reading "Barney McCabe" and then listening to it told by a black woman from South Carolina on *Moving Star Hall Singers*.

Sometimes very slight changes can make a story more comfortable to tell. For instance, Courlander's retellings seem uniformly choppy to me, though the plots are good. Since I find it feels natural to run sentences together more when I speak than when I write, I feel free to use many more "ands" than Courlander does, even in parts I memorize. In Carl Sandburg's "Kiss Me" I have replaced "the men who change the alphabets" with "the people who change the alphabets," which is more comfortable for me to use, yet it doesn't sound out of place.

When I think I have learned the story, I try telling it while doing something else—dishes, driving—so that I will get to know it well enough to overcome the distraction of seeing the audience. Different tellers use different distractions—telling to a mirror, telling with the radio on, telling to family, friends, neighbors, car pool. A live audience for rehearsals can substitute for a tape recorder in catching words or phrases that are not clear, either in enunciation or in meaning. If the story uses an unfamiliar word, and that word is vital to the understanding of the plot, I try to use a more familiar synonym in another sentence rather than sticking it in right after the unfamiliar word as a definition, which can sound stilted. Occasionally I will slip in a definition as I introduce the story. I don't like to replace the unfamiliar word entirely, as some of the fun of storytelling is enjoying the richness of the language.

At this point I am through with what is for me the bad part, learning the story; and I can get on to one of the better parts, learning to tell the story.

Telling a Story

AFTER I LEARN A STORY, I can start thinking about how to tell it. Why did this character say what she said? What was she thinking? How did she feel? What was she trying to convey to the other character? What do I want to emphasize about the story? Is it quiet, funny, scary? Can I make it more or less scary depending on how I tell it? Would I like to give the story special treatment . . . gestures the audience can follow in *Caps for Sale*? different voices for different characters in "The Three Bears"? a quiet, dreamy telling for "Umai"?

Starting a story at a walking pace will give room to speed up when the action gets exciting or to slow down for suspense or emphasis. Probably the commonest mistake is to tell too fast. This can be caused by nervousness or by lack of faith in the story and the listeners—a feeling that "most people have heard this or won't be interested so I can just get it over with quickly." If the teller believes in the story and gives it its due, even listeners who have heard the story will enjoy it again.

On the other hand, speaking too slowly, particularly drawing out a long word, can sometimes sound condescending—as though you don't think the audience can keep up with you. Listen to a Carl Sandburg record to find out how slowly a teller can speak and get away with it.

Along with pace, pauses are important in setting off one part of the story from another. A pause can build suspense: ". . . and back home that glass of milk . . . turn to blood." If a pause is too long, people might wonder if you have forgotten the next line. However, if you do need to search for a word, it is better to pause for a bit than to fill in with "uh" or with an apology. If you forget or make a mistake, just correct it without apology, as you do in everyday conversation. We are all used to people making mistakes when they talk, and we can even figure out what people really meant to say when they make a slip, don't hear it or don't think it's important, and so don't correct it. If you realize halfway through the story that you left out something important at the beginning, put it in as casually as possible—that has happened to every storyteller at one time or

another and no one will be unduly surprised.

Loudness can be used for emphasis at times, rather than pace or pauses, but must be used carefully. A small difference in volume will be quite noticeable, especially in a small room or a quiet story. A large increase can jolt your audience more than you meant to, while a large decrease can make the back row miss just the line you meant to emphasize. Again, a moderate volume to begin with will give scope for variation either way. At first you will have to enlist the help of your listeners to let you know whether you can be heard. With large audiences it is always good to check this, as there may be outside noises you are unaware of which are bothering the last few rows. On the other hand, loud telling can make an audience jumpy.

Whether or not you use gestures, and if so, how much, depends on how comfortable they feel to you; which, in turn, depends on how much you use them in conversation and how appropriate they seem to a particular story. I use lots of gestures in a straightforward story like *Caps for Sale* or "Lazy Jack" but hardly any when I tell a story rich in imagery like "Umai" or "Fiddler, Play Fast, Play Faster." And "lots" doesn't mean every possible gesture—I have seen tellers pantomime nearly every phrase, and look like mechanical toys.

I use different voices much less often than gestures; they come less naturally to me, and it's hard to remember to be consistent in giving each character a different accent or pitch unless the story itself reminds you, as "The Three Bears" does. And in most stories the characters are delineated more by what they say than by how they say it. This is not to say that they have to sound exactly the same—they may be conveying quite different emotions, but I can express them in my own voice, as I would if the emotions were my own. Tellers vary as to how much emotion they put into their voices in dialogue. I also vary the amount depending on the kind of story. Tall tales, for instance, can be told pretty deadpan. Certainly, when I listen to a tall tale, I don't like to hear the teller sound astonished. I want the audience reaction left to the audience.

Likewise, when I am the listener, I want to make my own judgment about the story or book that is being presented, and not have the teller usurp my role by breaking into the story line to remark "Isn't this a beautiful picture?" or by saying "Wasn't that a nice story?" at the end. I always resented fiercely the questions at the end of each chapter in school readers, so now I scrupulously avoid asking questions about a story at the end of the telling. I don't want to test the listeners' attention or understanding. However, especially with younger children, I do sometimes ask questions about their lives that relate to the story: after *In the Night Kitchen*, "Do you have cake for breakfast?"; after *There's a Nightmare in My Closet*, "Did you ever have a nightmare?"; but not "What did we learn from this story?" or "How many nightmares were in the closet?" Children like to tell you about themselves, and once the conversation is started, they may tell you their reaction to the story as well, if they feel like it.

It is natural for a teller to want immediate feedback on the performance and choice of story, but people don't always know immediately how they feel about any event, and can't always put their feelings into words when they do know. If you tell stories to the same group over a period of time, you find out that a child may stare out the window during the whole program and then go home and recite every story to a parent, or act out a favorite story in solitary play. Adults, unused to listening to stories, may take a while to decide that it's all right to enjoy them. But if you are telling to audiences that you won't see again, please take my assurance that this is so, and try not to put questions at the ends of chapters.

There is no rule that says a teller must meet the eye of each listener during the course of a story, but if you look mostly at the floor or ceiling, the audience could get the idea that you are afraid of them or not interested in them. I look around a lot at different faces, because I feel that looking at just a few people puts a burden on them to look interested. Of course

my eye is drawn back most often to those faces that do look most interested, but with children it is prudent to give some attention to the restless ones, because it may keep them from getting so wriggly that they bother their neighbors. Cynthia Orr, a teller in Oregon, tells stories with her eyes closed from time to time, so she can react just to the words and not to the audience. She says she and her listeners both find this relaxing. I tried it and found it totally distracting, because I had to make a physical effort to keep my eyes closed. But it is interesting to try; you might like it. If you don't, you can still let your listeners know that it's okay to close their eyes during a quiet story if they want to.

I was present when Ray Hicks, a North Carolina farmer and wildcrafter who is also a fine storyteller, told a Jack tale to an audience of about three hundred at the National Storytelling Festival in Jonesboro. Like most tellers, he is probably accustomed to telling to twenty-five people or less. What he did was to maintain eye contact with about twenty-five people in the front center of the audience, while the rest of us, instead of having a story told to us, watched him tell the story to that group, watched them react to it, and saw him enjoy their reactions. It worked.

A little nervousness is not a bad thing; it keeps me on my toes, alert to the audience and listening to the story, so I don't lose my place. The trick is to not show the nervousness. The problem is that you don't always know how you show it. I didn't know how I showed mine until I saw a film of myself—I lick my lips. A film or your best friend will tell you what you do—twist your feet, wring your hands, say "uh" at the beginning of every phrase, clear your throat, brush your hair out of your eyes. Once you are aware of your habit, you can work on breaking it (or get a haircut).

I don't always enjoy a story the first time I tell it to an audience. This may mean it's not a good story for me, but it is more likely that I am just not used to telling it yet, or that I have not found the right audience for it. I need many tellings to become really comfortable with some stories. I also depend on audience reaction and my feelings as I tell a story to let me know if I should cut it or extend it, ham it up or tell it straight. A student in one of my classes said she had read somewhere about "having the patience to do something badly" and this is certainly necessary in practicing and beginning to tell a story. So don't lose heart—it gets better.

Someone said of a certain writer of young adult novels that she wrote dialogue not the way teenagers talk, but the way they like to think they talk. And when I tell a story, I usually try to sound not like somebody else, but like me at my best, without the "uhs" and "you knows" that spatter everyday conversation, and without the bright cheerfulness that comes over even the most sensible people when they talk to the very young. Of course, if you want to present a folktale as something that happened to you, as many tellers do, then you will want to leave more "everydayness" in your speech to sound more convincing.

The sense of sounding like myself develops over a period of time. I started out trying to follow my storytelling teacher's instructions, and ten years later, with my partner's help, became aware of this and learned to act as much like myself during the story as I do during my introduction of it. I still pick up some of the style of the teller if I learn a story directly from another person or from a record rather than from a book. Sometimes I like this, and keep it; sometimes I don't like it, and put more of my own voice in the telling as I repeat the story.

I have given you my ideas on how to tell a story. The decision on how *you* will tell any story is, finally, a matter of taste, of personal style, of experience, and of being aware of your listeners—that you neither bore them with monotone voice, nor embarrass them with overacting, nor overshadow their response to the story with your own.

Knowledge of your material can help you make decisions about performing it, so I have listed some readings about folklore as well as storytelling at the end of this chapter. When I tell a folktale in my own words, I try to say things in a way that is not completely foreign to the time and place the story comes from. The less I know about a culture, the more reluctant I am to change anything in a story. For instance, I ad lib a lot when I do *It Could Always Be Worse* as a tandem story, but I have to remind non-Jewish partners *not* to have the rabbi suggest that the man bring his pig into the house, as the rabbi would not expect him to have a pig.

BOOKS ON STORYTELLING

Hamlet's speech to the players (Act III, Scene 2) is an excellent brief statement on technique that applies as well to storytelling as to acting.

Baker, Augusta, and Ellin Green. *Storytelling: Art and Technique.* Bowker, 1977. Basic information on learning and oral telling, plus a history of storytelling in libraries and an appendix on how to set up a storytelling workshop. The chapters on learning and telling are summarized in the March 1978 *School Library Journal.*

Bauer, Caroline Feller. *Handbook for Storytellers.* American Library Ass'n., 1977. Media-oriented. Instructions on making flannelboards, telling stories on radio and TV, publicity for library programs. "Other Literary Sources" (pp. 134–136) includes good ideas for finding stories to tell to adults.

Colum, Padraic. *Story Telling, New and Old.* Macmillan, 1968 (c. 1927). The whole thing in a nutshell.

Colwell, Eileen. *A Storyteller's Choice.* Walck, 1964. The stories are rather difficult, but the notes on how to tell (and sometimes cut) each story are illuminating. General discussion of storytelling pp. 203–208.

Cook, Elizabeth. *The Ordinary and the Fabulous: An Introduction to Myths, Legends and Fairy Tales for Teachers and Storytellers.* Cambridge University Press, 2nd edition, 1976. Good for comparing different versions of myths.

DeWit, Dorothy. *Children's Faces Looking Up.* American Library Association, 1979. How to condense, expand, or retell a story; suggestions for theme programs.

Foster, Joanna. *How to Conduct Effective Picture Book Programs.* Westchester Library System, 1967. This pamphlet is useful for beginners or volunteers, with or without the film, *The Pleasure Is Mutual,* for which it was written.

Horne, Catherine. *Word Weaving: A Storytelling Workbook.* Word Weaving, P.O. Box 5646, San Francisco, CA 94101, 1980. Instructions in one storytelling method, stories arranged in order of difficulty, and ideas for using stories in the classroom.

Johnson, Edna. *Anthology of Children's Literature.* Houghton-Mifflin, any edition. Excellent appendix, "Storytelling," with bibliography on storytelling (and a wealth of good stories and poems in the body of the book).

Pellowski, Anne. *The World of Storytelling.* Bowker, 1977. The chapters on "Folk Storytelling" and "Style, Gesture, and Voice Change" show the range of variation between and within cultures in different parts of the world. The paragraphs on "The Art of Listening" on page 177 give excellent advice to any teller, anywhere.

Sawyer, Ruth. *How to Tell a Story.* Reprint from Compton's Encyclopedia, 1963. A legendary storyteller tells how in ten pages.

Sawyer, Ruth. *The Way of the Storyteller.* Viking, 1942. To the above, this adds excellent background on a storyteller's life, art, and sources. Watch out for the masculine representing both genders—there are medicine-women as well as medicine-men in traditional societies; there were female troubadours as well as male.

Shedlock, Marie L. *The Art of the Storyteller.* Dover, 3rd edition 1951 (c. 1915) Dated on choosing but still the best on technique. Try chapters 1, 2, 3 and 7.

Ziskind, Sylvia. *Telling Stories to Children.* Wilson, 1976. The useful part is chapter 3, "Mastering Technique" (pp. 26–41), which includes voice exercises, diction, dialects, props and gestures, interruptions.

STORYTELLERS ON RECORDS

For stories that are not read or recited by actors, but told by tellers, send for the Catalog of Storytelling Resources from NAPPS, P.O. Box 112, Jonesboro, TN 37659. They carry many excellent records, including the Folktellers (Connie Regan and Barbara Freeman), Marshall Dodge, Ray Hicks, Laura Simms, Diane Wolkstein, David Holt and Linda Goss, and tapes by Jackie Torrance and Cynthia Orr. Other storytelling records and music records which include telling are:

Birds, Beast, Bugs and Bigger Fishes. Pete Seeger. Folkways FC 7011. 43 W. 61st Street, New York, NY 10023. "The Foolish Frog."

Jack Tales (II). Mrs. Maud Long of Hot Springs, NC. Library of Congress, Folklore of the United States series.

Moving Star Hall Singers. Folkways FS 3841. "Barney McCabe."

Richard Chase Tells Three "Jack" Tales from the Southern Appalachians. Folk-Legacy FTA-6.

Plum Pudding: Stories and Songs with Nancy Schimmel and the Plum City Players. Sisters' Choice, 2027 Parker Street, Berkeley, CA 94704.

Rootagaba Stories. Carl Sandburg. Caedmon TC 1089. 505 Eighth Avenue, NY 10018.

Some Mountain Tales About Jack. Billy Edd Wheeler. Spoken Arts SA 1113. 310 North Avenue, New Rochelle, NY 10801.

A Storyteller's Journey. Penninah Schram. Pom Records, Suite 8c, 525 West End Avenue, New York, NY 10024.

STORYTELLERS ON FILM AND VIDEO

Fixin' to Tell About Jack. 25 minutes, color, 16mm. Appalshop. Box 743, Whitesburg, KY 41858. Ray Hicks telling "Soldier Jack" in a North Carolina accent so thick, Yankees need to read the story first in Richard Chase's *The Jack Tales* (Houghton, 1971) or get the script from Appalshop. Good, though.

NAPPS (P.O. Box 112, Jonesboro, TN 37659) has videotapes of traditional and modern tellers such as the incomparable Jackie Torrance, for rent or for viewing at their National Storytelling Resource Center in Jonesboro.

SAVES Videotapes (Southern Appalachian Video Ethnography Series) of Kathryn Tucker Windham (ghost stories) and Marshall Ward (Jack tales and others. Broadside Video. Elm & Millard, Johnson City, TN 37601.

STORYTELLERS: LIVE

National Directory of Storytellers. NAPPS, Box 112, Jonesboro, TN 37659. Where to find Michael Parent, Maggi Peirce, Cynthia Orr, and about 150 other tellers. Includes address, phone, specialties, fees, references. NAPPS also puts on the National Storytelling Festival in Jonesboro on the first full weekend in October; their newsletter, *The Yarnspinner,* included in the yearly membership of $15, lists other festivals around the country.

Storytelling Hotline. Call the New England Storytelling Center, (617) 868-9600 ext. 449, for a recorded listing of storytelling events in the Boston area. They also have workshops, concerts, quarterly calendar. 29 Everett St., Cambridge, MA 02238.

The Folktellers—Connie Regan and Barbara Freeman. P.O. Box 2898, Asheville, NC 28802. Programs and workshops across the country. Featured in the November 1978 *School Library Journal* and July 1980 *New Age.* Two records and a bibliography available.

Sisters' Choice—Nancy Schimmel, 2027 Parker Street, Berkeley, CA 94704. (415) 843-0533. Programs and workshops across the country. *The Handsome Prince* (Franciscan Films). *Plum Pudding* (see Storytellers on Records).

ON FOLKLORE AND FAIRY TALES

Serious but not impenetrable articles and books.

Family Folklore. Smithsonian Institution, 1976. Pantheon, 1982. Family anecdotes selected from stories collected from people attending the Smithsonian's annual Folklife Festival.

Kirschenblatt-Gimblett, Barbara. "A Parable in Context: A Social Interactional Analysis of Storytelling Performance," in *Folklore: Performance and Communication,* ed. Dan Ben-Amos and Kenneth S. Goldstein. Mouton, 1975. Using a folktale to make a point in a social situation.

Sexton, Anne. *Transformations.* Houghton, 1971. Psychological implications of Grimm tales explored in poetry. Briefer and more convincing (to me) than Bettelheim's *The Uses of Enchantment.*

Shah, Idries. *World Tales.* Harcourt, 1979. Each story is introduced by a brief sketch of its history and travels, literary connections, philosophical or psychological connotations, etc.

Stone, Kay. "Things Walt Disney Never Told Us," *Journal of American Folklore 88,* Jan. 1975, pp. 42–50, critique pp. 103–4. Role of women in the most popularized fairy tales. This is a special issue of *JAF* on women in folklore. It has been reprinted by the University of Texas Press as *Women and Folklore,* Claire R. Farrer, ed.

Toelken, Barre. "Folklore, Worldview and Communication," in *Folklore: Performance and Communication,* ed. Dan Ben-Amos. Helps explain why linear-oriented WASPs have difficulty appreciating folktales from circular-oriented Native American cultures.

Tolkien, J. R. R. *Tree and Leaf.* "On Fairy Tales," pp. 3–84. An essay on the "sub-creation" of fantasy worlds with their own rules, whose workings reflect values in our own world.

Wolkstein, Diane. *The Magic Orange Tree and Other Haitian Folktales.* Knopf, 1978. Each story is introduced by a description of the circumstances under which Wolkstein collected it—who was telling, to whom, how, and what the audience reaction was.

PERIODICALS

Fabula, Journal of Folktale Studies. 3/yr, 1958 + . Berlin.

Journal of American Folklore, q., 1888 + . American Folklore Society. Indexed in Humanities Index.

The Laugh-makers. 6/yr., 1982 + . 108 Berwyn Ave., Syracuse, NY 13210. A magazine for adults who perform for children; has a regular column on storytelling.

New York Folklore Quarterly. 1944 + . New York Folklore Society. Look for articles by Ben Botkin.

Parabola—Myth and the Quest for Meaning. q., 1976 + . Society for the Study of Myth and Tradition, 150 Fifth Ave., New York, NY 10011. Especially "Storytelling and Education," Vol. 4, no. 4 (1979), entire issue, and "Telling Stories, a Conversation with Diane Wolkstein and Paul Jordan-Smith," Vol. 2, no. 4 (1977), pp. 82–91.

BIBLIOGRAPHY

Storytelling Center of Oneonta, P.O. Box 297, Oneonta, NY 13820, has available an extensive (though not annotated) bibliography of books and articles on many aspects of storytelling—technique, use in therapy and education, etc.

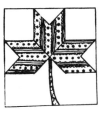

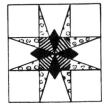

Choosing the Medium

PEOPLE ASK IF I USE A-V (audio-visual aids) when I tell stories. The answer is no and yes. They are usually referring to something that plugs in—a projector or record player—and I don't use them. However, the audience does hear me tell the story, and does see my facial expressions and gestures, so I am an audio-visual device myself, though I don't need to be plugged in. Some of my stories are more A-V than others, and I will discuss here some of the media that storytellers can use to put variety into a storytelling session or to attract attention in a distracting situation.

Many tellers begin by reading stories aloud, with or without showing the pictures. All that applies to telling applies here—phrasing, pace, even some eye contact—so ideally the story should be rehearsed, even though it is not learned or memorized. A pitfall in reading aloud is launching into a sentence and then realizing you have put the emphasis on the wrong word. Only a rehearsal—even a silent one—can prevent this.

Tellers disagree about showing pictures with a story. Some prefer to leave the illustration of the story to the listeners' imagination (which they feel is all too rarely exercised) and then they show the pictures afterward or not at all. Some stories are so rich in language, imagery, ideas, that adding a visual element would only take away from the aural experience. Bettelheim* adds that a monster imagined by the listener may have useful psychological meaning, while the illustrator's monster "may scare us without evoking any deeper meaning beyond anxiety." Others feel that the picture book program is an opportunity to introduce young children to excellent art, and want to show the pictures right along with the story.

When I was doing two pre-school story hours a week, I used a lot of stories with pictures because it seemed the easiest thing to do. Now, I try to let my feeling about the book determine how I will present

it. Some, like *Rosie's Walk*, have half the story in the pictures and can't be used without them. Others, like *Mommy, Buy Me a China Doll*, are long and repetitious, which is fine for bedtime, but may fall flat in storytime without the added interest of the pictures. Some, like *Whose Mouse Are You?*, I do with the pictures just because I like them (the illustrations in this one appeal as much to a high school child-development class as to a pre-school storytime).

It is best to practice reading and showing picture books in front of a mirror or a friend to see if the pictures really can be seen. Common faults are holding the book at a slant so the pictures are aimed mainly at the ceiling, covering parts of the picture with fingers, and going too fast, especially if the text is brief. Also check for pitfalls like a picture oriented end-ways in an otherwise side-ways book, or a picture that gives away the punch line before you get to it in the text—this last may require memorizing a line or two to permit you to turn the page at the proper moment.

If your public library, school district, or a nearby college has the film *The Pleasure Is Mutual* (24 mins., color. Children's Book Council, 1967), try to see it. Though dated, it will show you more about using picture books than I can tell you.

But picture books needn't always be used as they are in the film, where every picture is shown as the story is read. I do *Caps for Sale* without the pictures partly because I don't care for the pictures, but mostly because I like to make it an audience participation story. I shake my fist at the monkeys, and the audience, with only the slightest encouragement, shakes its fists at the peddler. There are other books I would use without the pictures because the pictures are too small or delicate to be seen at a distance, or because I feel they are sexist or racist—defects more common to illustrations than to the texts they illustrate. On the other hand, I read *Sam* with the pictures, because they show a black child in a story that all children can identify with.

And then there are a few stories, like *Three Billy Goats Gruff*, that go over well in any medium, and are in such demand that a variety of media does

---

The Uses of Enchantment: The Meaning and Importance of Fairy Tales by Bruno Bettelheim (Knopf, 1976), pp. 59-60.

more to prevent boredom in the teller than in the listener. There's a book with large, bold, appealing, not-too-scary illustrations by Marcia Brown, and the story lends itself to puppets, pantomime, and creative dramatics. It is perfect for finger puppets: The left hand is the bridge and the left arm the hillside. The troll puppet, on the left thumb, hides under the bridge and pops up at the "up" of "gobble you up!" The goats are played by the first, middle and little fingers of the right hand (ring fingers are not nimble enough to play goats).

The Fat Cat has illustrations I love, but I have been won away by another method of telling. I narrate the story and play the woodcutter. My accomplice, with a sheet tied around her neck, plays the cat and chooses the rest of the cast from the audience, while I coach them. In a few minutes we are ready to start. As I narrate the story, the players one by one recite their one line, "What have you been eating, my little cat? You are so fat!" One by one the cat tells them what she has already eaten and then "eats" them by throwing the sheet over them. Older children always cooperate spontaneously, though we never tell them what is going to happen. Younger ones should be at the end of the line so they are not surprised, and may need some coaxing from the friendly cat. If they don't go in, or if they come out again to see what the cat looks like, that is part of the fun.

Margo Zemach's *It Could Always Be Worse* (Farrar Straus, 1977) can be dramatized even more simply than *The Fat Cat*, and there's no danger of frightening even the youngest participants. I am the narrator and the man whose house was too small. An accomplice, with very little preparation, is the rabbi. The children are brought on stage, as the story progresses, to be the family and the animals, doing sound effects, of course. I say "he ran out of the house and slammed the door" and clap or stamp to cue the children to stop the sound effects while I talk to the rabbi. I would do only one of these on-stage participation stories in a program, and put it near the end, as they are pretty heady stuff. They are especially good for family programs.

A more refined kind of dramatized storytelling is tandem telling. The first tandem storytelling I heard was at the Jonesboro festival, in 1975, from the Roadside Theater and from the Folktellers. It is a form halfway between telling and dramatization. Two (or more) tellers alternate narrating a story, and take different characters' parts during dialogue. It is not a play, because there is still much narration, and there need be no props or costumes and very little

movement beyond the gestures tellers would use anyway. It is more theatrical than solo telling, however, and is well suited to provide variety and excitement in a stage program such as a school assembly. By eliminating a lot of "he said" and "she said" it can step up the pace of a story. At its best it sounds like two friends so eager to tell you something that they are interrupting each other. In fact, it is best done by friends whose style is similar enough to blend into one narration.

The stories that best translate into tandem telling either have two main characters ("Ticoumba and the President," Arnold Lobel's Frog and Toad stories, Zemach's *Penny a Look*), or one main character who interacts with a series of minor characters one at a time, as in Toby Talbot's *Bucketful of Moon* (Lothrop, 1976), "The Gingerbread Boy" or "The Pancake."

Flannelboard is a popular storytelling medium, but takes time to prepare well, so the stories should be chosen with care. Cloth or felt cut-out figures will stick to a board covered with flannel, so figures can be re-drawn enlarged from a book too small to use with a group, and displayed on the board as they come into the narrative. This works best with cumulative stories or songs, where the figures can be added and/or taken off in succession, or for stories with a *very* simple cast and plot. Otherwise the teller has to pay more attention to the board than to the telling or the audience. I don't use flannelboards, so if you want to know more, see Caroline Bauer's *Handbook for Storytellers*.

Another way of presenting stories is by singing them. Some folktales have parallels in ballads: "The Husband Who Was to Mind the House" (*Womenfolk and Fairy Tales*) is echoed in the ballad "Equinoctial and Phoebe." They can be used successfully in the same program. Ballads can be used on their own or as introductions to books in which they are illustrated or retold in prose (Joseph Jacobs has retold several).

You don't need a great voice or perfect pitch to sing in story programs. A simple instrument such as an autoharp can help you stay on key, or you can sing along with a record. (Just playing a record without singing along won't encourage audience participation, though it's all right for background music before the program starts.) Young children are a good audience to start on. They aren't too critical about tone or pitch; they respond mainly to rhythm. If you aren't holding an instrument, you can choose a picture-book song and show the pictures as you sing. A song or chant with hand motions can be a welcome break in a story hour, when children get wiggly and your arms are cramped from holding up a picture book.

These are some of the different ways in which a story can be told. No storyteller needs to know all of them. Many tellers prefer straight oral telling and they need nothing more. I like to have a choice of media ready for special occasions.

Which medium to use depends on the audience as well as the story or the book format. A small audience enjoys straight telling, finger puppets, and picture books. A large audience will respond to participation stories as well as to straight telling, to larger books, and to hand puppets used without a stage. For a very large audience, books will not do. If attention-getting devices are needed, they will

have to be flannelboards, large puppets, dramatized storytelling such as *The Fat Cat*, and shadowplays. I don't usually do a whole program with props unless the audience is large, unruly, and unused to storytelling. Generally, even in a distracting situation like an outdoor fair I can do a few visual stories to attract an audience and focus attention, and then do some oral telling as well.

Whether you ever use props with storytelling depends also on what feels comfortable to you. Some beginners find that a guitar or a string trick gives them something to do with their hands and makes them feel easier about facing an audience. Others find props just something extra to think about when they would rather concentrate on the telling.

SIMPLE PICTURE BOOKS

Brown, Margaret Wise. *Goodnight Moon*, illus. Clement Hurd. Harper, 1947, pbk. 1977.

Burningham, John. *Mr. Gumpy's Outing*. Holt, 1971.

Ginsburg, Mirra. *The Chick and the Duckling*, illus. Jose Aruego. Macmillan, 1972.

Hutchins, Pat. *Rosie's Walk*. Macmillan, 1968, pbk. 1971.

Kraus, Robert. *Whose Mouse Are You?* illus. Jose Aruego. Macmillan, 1970, pbk. 1972.

Parker, Nancy Winslow. *Poofy Loves Company*. Dodd, Mead, 1980.

Rockwell, Harlow. *My Doctor*. Macmillan, 1973.

Sendak, Maurice. The Nutshell Library: *Alligators All Around, Chicken Soup with Rice, One Was Johnny, Pierre*. Harper, 1962.

Wheeler, Cindy. *A Good Day, A Good Night*. Lippincott, 1980.

Williams, Garth. *The Chicken Book: A Traditional Rhyme*. Delacorte, 1970.

LONGER PICTURE BOOKS

Asbjornsen, P. C. *The Three Billy Goats Gruff*, illus. Marcia Brown. Harcourt, 1957, pbk. 1972.

Bemelmens, Ludwig. *Madeline*. Viking, 1939, Penguin pbk. 1977.

Flack, Marjorie. *Angus and the Cat*. Doubleday, 1971.

Gag, Wanda. *Millions of Cats*. Coward, 1928, pbk. 1977.

Kent, Jack. *The Fat Cat: A Danish Folktale*. Parents, 1971, Scholastic pbk. 1972.

Marshall, James. *George and Martha*. Houghton, 1972, pbk. 1974.

Mayer, Mercer. *There's a Nightmare in My Closet*. Dial, 1968, pbk. 1976.

Minarik, Else. *A Kiss for Little Bear*, illus. Maurice Sendak. Harper, 1968.

Mosel, Arlene. *Tikki Tikki Tembo*, illus. Blair Lent. Holt, 1968.

Scott, N. H. *Sam*, illus. Symeon Shimin. McGraw, 1967.

Segal, Lore. *All the Way Home*, illus. James Marshall. Farrar, 1973.

Sendak, Maurice. *In the Night Kitchen*. Harper, 1970. *Where the Wild Things Are*. Harper, 1963.

Zemach, Harve. *Mommy, Buy Me a China Doll*, illus. Margot Zemach. Farrar, 1966. *The Judge: An Untrue Tale*. Farrar, 1969.

PARTICIPATION PICTURE BOOKS

Elting, Mary, and Michael Folsom. *Q is for Duck, An Alphabet Guessing Game*, illus. Jack Kent. Houghton, 1980.

Hill, Eric. *Where's Spot?* Putnam, 1980.

Hoban, Tana. *Count and See*. Macmillan, 1972, pbk. 1974. *Look Again*. Macmillan, 1971.

Shaw, Charles. *It Looked Like Spilt Milk*. Harper, 1947.

PICTURE BOOKS TO SING

Fiddle-I-Fee, A Traditional American Chant, illus. Diane Stanley. Little, Brown, 1979. Music not included, but it can be found in *The Fireside Song Book of Birds and Beasts*, ed. Jane Yolen. Simon & Schuster, 1972.

The Fox Went Out on a Chilly Night, illus. Peter Spier. Doubleday, 1961.

Hush Little Baby, illus. Aliki. Prentice-Hall, 1968.

Shannon, George. *Lizard's Song*, illus. Jose Aruego and Ariane Dewey. Greenwillow, 1981.

SONGBOOKS

Reynolds, Malvina. *There's Music in the Air, Songs for the Middle-Young.* Schroder Music, 1976. 2027 Parker Street, Berkeley, CA 94704. Intelligent songs for eight- to thirteen-year-olds on many topics, including ecology. *Tweedles and Foodles for Young Noodles.* Schroder, 1961. For younger children.

Seeger, Ruth Crawford. *American Folk Songs for Children.* Doubleday, 1948. Folk songs and how to use them with children, presented by a composer, teacher and folklorist.

Sendak, Maurice. *Maurice Sendak's Really Rosie Starring the Nutshell Kids.* Music by Carole King. Harper, 1975. These songs from the TV special and film can be used with the Nutshell Library.

Winn, Marie. *The Fireside Book of Children's Songs,* Simon & Schuster, 1966. The good old nursery songs and camp songs.

Yurchenko, Henrietta. *A Fiesta of Folksongs from Spain and Latin America.* Putnam, 1967. Bilingual, with both free and literal translations and pronunciation.

RECORDS

American Folk Songs for Children. Sung by Pete Seeger from Ruth Crawford Seeger's book. Folkways FTS 31501. 43 W. 61st Street, New York, NY 10023.

Funnybugs, Giggleworms, and Other Good Friends. Composed and sung by Malvina Reynolds. Pacific Cascade LPS 7025. Vida, OR 97488. Also her *Artichokes, Griddlecakes and Other Good Things.* Singable pre-school songs.

Magical Songs. Sung by Malvina Reynolds, from her book *There's Music in the Air.* Cassandra CR 040. 2027 Parker Street, Berkeley, CA 94704. School-age songs for singing, dancing, and thinking.

Old Mother Hippletoe: Rural and Urban Children's Songs. New World Records NW 291. Folk sources of children's songs (mostly sung by adults) and singing games (sung by children). Discography and list of videotapes of children's games.

Our Record. Tom Hunter and Friends. Long Sleeve Records, 22 Eugene, Mill Valley, CA 94941. Child's-eye view of light and heavy subjects.

Really Rosie. Composed and sung by Carole King, words from Maurice Sendak's Nutshell Library. Ode PE 34945, PET 34945.

Spin, Spider, Spin. Composed and sung by Marcia Berman and Patty Zeitlin. Educational Activities AR 551. Freeport, NY 11520. Friendly songs about snakes, bugs, etc. Also their other records on this label.

Through Children's Eyes. Sung by The Limelighters. RCA LPM/LSP-2512. Includes my favorite participation song, "Join into the Game."

We All Have a Song: Activity and Bed-time Songs with Ginni Clemens. Folkways FC 7576. An audience-participation record. Try it.

Whoever Shall Have Some Good Peanuts, and Other Folksongs for Children. Sung by Sam Hinton. Folkways FC 7530.

Lirica Infantil. Sung in Spanish by José-Luis Orozco. Babel, 255 E. 14th St., Oakland, CA 94606. Easy-to-lead songs, chants and singing games from Latin America. Lyrics and translations included.

FINGERPUPPETS

Mrs. Jac Thorpe, 2085 Jefferson Drive, Hattiesburg, MS 39401. Send for price list for puppets and patterns. These knit puppets of story characters are easy to use because they cling to the fingers.

An Assortment of Stories

I learned "Barney McCabe," a *cante fable* (story with a song in it), from Guy Carawan, who learned it from Mrs. Janie Hunter on John's Island, South Carolina. Since the book in which it appears is out of print, Guy gave me permission to reprint it here. He accompanies himself as he sings; I sing *a cappella* but teach Jack and Mary's song to most of the audience and Barney McCabe's to the back row before I start. I tell it in my own words rather than trying to reproduce the regional speech.

"Barney McCabe" is related to an African story, "Tsimbarumé the Hardened Bachelor," retold by Hugh Tracey in *The Lion on the Path* (London, Routledge and Kegan Paul, Ltd., 1967). Tsimbarumé, a hunter, follows a young woman down a hole into another world, where she is held captive by a witch. The witch tricks Tsimbarumé into a tree, then starts to chop down the tree with her tooth. He calls his three dogs with a magic song. They attack the witch, but she kills them with her tooth. The song is so powerful that it brings the dogs to life again and they finish off the witch.

I usually follow "Barney McCabe" with Bonnie Lockhart's "Witch Song" (*Plum Pudding*, Sisters' Choice Records, 1982), which presents a more positive view of witches as herbal healers, midwives, and storytellers.

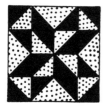

I made up "A Story for Heather" as I drove down the Blue Ridge Parkway after a visit with the Carawans, whose daughter's name is Heather. I passed a turnoff to the town of Crossnore and began to wonder what a crossnore was. The story is the answer. It contains no songs or visual elements. Crossnores don't like them.

Of the two visual stories that follow "Barney McCabe," the first, "The Rainhat," is traditional; I have seen three versions. I learned mine from a girl, about nine, who was telling it to the librarian when I dropped into a library in San Francisco. I changed the boy in her story to a girl, as I wasn't finding enough girls in children's adventure stories, but I told the story for many months before I realized I was saying "fireman's helmet" instead of "firefighter's helmet." The same folds, without the story, can be found in H. A. Rey's *Curious George Rides a Bike* (Houghton, 1952, pbk. 1973). A small group of first graders or a class of second graders can learn these folds, or most of them.

The second visual story, "The Handsome Prince," I made up to go with traditional Chinese folds taught to me by Elizabeth Sor when I worked with her at the San Mateo County Library. The instructions following the story show the figures in succession as they appear in the story. This story is difficult for one person to fold and tell at the same time; Elizabeth and I did it together for fifteen branch libraries before I was able to do it alone. For this reason, I made a film of the story (Franciscan Films). I use the film or the live story to introduce the art of Chinese and Japanese (origami) paperfolding to children from third grade up. For third grade, I don't teach all the figures in the film.

If you want to go on with paperfolding, which is a good craft for libraries as it is clean and requires no equipment and not much space, here are some easy-to-teach figures:

The Art of Origami: Paper Folding, Traditional and Modern by Samuel Randlett. Dutton, 1961. See waterbomb, salt cellar (fortuneteller).

Folding Paper Toys by Shari Lewis. Stein & Day, 1963. See bugcatcher (fortuneteller), house and couch and bureau. The jumping frog is not easy, but recycles old catalog cards.

Origami Toys by Toshie Takahama. Japan Publications Trading Co., 1255 Howard Street, San Francisco, CA 94103. See ko-tong-kong, "The Captain's Shirt" (a version of "The Rainhat"), leaping frog (slightly simpler than Lewis'). Also includes finger puppets.

Traditional origami paper is cut exactly square, white on one side and colored on the other. It is helpful for teaching and satisfying to use. It is available from The Origami Center of America, 31 Union Square, New York, NY 10003, which also carries origami books. Send large stamped, self-addressed envelope for their price list.

Other good visual stories are "The Yam Thief," a string trick story good for catching the attention of older children dubious about listening to stories, and *The Wild Ducks and the Goose,* my favorite chalkboard story, which appears in different versions in *On the Banks of Plum Creek* by Laura Ingalls Wilder

(p. 318), *Bushbabies* by William Stevenson (p. 198), and Karen Blixen's *Out of Africa.*

To me, the most fascinating and beautiful visual storytelling is signed storytelling for the deaf. If you can find someone who signs and has time to practice with you, you can do a program of interest to both hearing and deaf audiences. The practice beforehand is necessary for three reasons: the signer can do a more creative interpretation if he or she is familiar wih the story, you can adjust your pace to the needs of the signer, and you won't be so distracted by the signing if your curiosity is satisfied during rehearsal.

"The Pancake" is an old Norwegian nursery tale that appears in several collections. Gay Ducey and I have re-worked it for tandem telling (as described in "Choosing the Medium"). Dialogue is in roman type, narration in italic. Pace is particularly important in this story. We start easy, then speed up a lot and overlap in the chase scene, ease off for the transition, overlap some in the dialogue, slow for the exchange with the pig, and eat the pancake as quickly as possible.

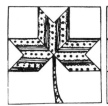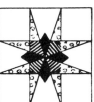

BARNEY McCABE

Once upon a time it was a twin sister and brother. The sister name was Mary and the brother name was Jack. One day they decided to go on a long traveling. But Jack was a wise child and he told Mary to go in the house and ask Mother could we go. Her mother say, "Yes, you could go, but take care." So Jack say, "Wait a minute, Sister," and went to the barn and get four grain of corn. And Mary said to Jack, "What you gonna do with that corn?" Jack said, "In a long while, you will see." So he put the corn in his pocket.

Then before he leave home Jack told his mother, say, "Mama, I got three dogs—Barney McCabe, Doodle-le-doo and Soo-Boy. I going to leave a glass of milk on the table. If you see that glass of milk turn to blood, I want you to turn my dogs loose."

So they went on traveling and all the time wondering what was the end going to be. Pretty soon it come dark and they begin to get weary. They knocked at an old lady house. The old lady run to the door, say, "Who is it?"

Jack say, "Me, Mama. Could we spend the night here? 'Cause we far from home and we very tired." Old lady say, "Oh yes, come on in."

All that time she was a witch-craft and the children didn't know it. She fed them and put them to bed. She had a knife she call "Tommy Hawk." After she put the children to bed she began to sharpen it up:

Children say, "Grandma, what's all that noise? We can't sleep."

She say, "That ain't nothing but your grandma frock-tail switchin' to get your supper hot. You all go back to sleep."

So Jack begin to wonder how they can get out of there. Then he remember the old lady have a room full of pumpkin. Jack takes two pumpkin and put 'em in the bed and cover 'em over, pretend it was he and his sister. Then Jack throw one grain of corn to the window, and it turn into a ladder. Jack and Mary climbed the ladder down and they start traveling for home.

The old lady sharpen her knife faster:

> "Penny, get your knife,
> Penny, get your knife,
> Penny, get your knife, go shock 'em, shock 'em.
>
> Hump back a Josie back a see Antony,
> Mama and your daddy tell me so,
> See so, I think it so
> Tam-a-ram-a-ram."

She didn't hear no noise, so she sneak in the room and chop up the pumpkins in the bed. Then she ran in the kitchen and got a dishpan, and pull back the cover. And when she think she putting the meat in the pan for cook for breakfast, she drop the pumpkin in the pan. And Jack and Mary was long gone.

She get mad, grab Tommy Hawk and flew down on those children. The children drop another grain of corn and it turn a tall pine tree. And Jack and Mary flew up in that tree. The old lady start cut on the tree, say:

Then Jack drop a grain of corn down from the pine tree, and back home that glass of milk turn to blood. Them dogs begin to holler. Jack's mother ran in the yard and turned the dogs loose. Jack say:

Dogs say:

Old witch say:

"A chip on the old block, a chip on the new block,
A chip on the old block, a chip on the new block."

Every time she chip, the tree lean and lean. Jack call:

"Barney McCabe, and Doodle-le-doo, and Soo-Boy,
Your maussa almost gone."

Dogs say:

"Maussa, Maussa, coming all the time,
Maussa, Maussa, coming all the time."

Jack drop another corn, the last corn, and it turn a bridge. And then when the old witch pull the ax up for take the last chop and chop Jack and Mary in the head, the dogs ran up. Barney McCabe cut her throat, Doodle-le-doo suck her blood and Soo-Boy drag her on the bridge, the bridge bend and that's the way that story end.

THE RAINHAT

ONCE THERE WAS A LITTLE GIRL who wanted to go outside to play. But her mother wouldn't let her, because it was raining so hard. The little girl didn't want to play inside, because all she had to play with was one piece of paper. So she took the paper and folded it, and folded it, waiting for the rain to stop, but it didn't stop, so she folded the paper some more, and she made herself a rainhat, and put it on, and went outside anyway.

When she got outside, she saw a house burning down, and she wanted to help put out the fire. So she took off her rainhat, and folded it, and folded it, and made herself a firefighter's helmet. Then she went to help put out the fire. She poured on water, and poured on water, until the fire was all out. But the rain kept coming down, and she poured on so much water besides, that there was a flood.

The little girl wanted to go sailing on the flood. But she wouldn't go sailing in a firefighter's hat, so she took it off, and folded it, and made a pirate hat. Then she was all ready to go sailing . . . except . . . she needed a boat. So she took off her pirate hat, and folded it, and folded it, and made a boat. Then she was ready to go sailing. But the flood had covered up lots of things, and the little girl couldn't see them, so she ran right into a car and broke the bow of the boat. She turned the boat around and went right on sailing. Then she ran into a house, and broke the stern off the boat, but she was a brave little girl, and she went on sailing. Then she ran into a library, and broke a hole right in the middle of the boat. Well, with a hole right in the middle of the boat, what happened to the boat?* It sank. But the little girl didn't drown, because she was wearing a life jacket.

---

*Here is an exception to an otherwise reliable rule: Never ask a question during a story, you will always get an irrelevant reply. But somehow this question always (knock wood) elicits the right response.

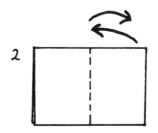

fold rectangular

paper in half

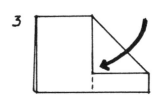

open rainhat,
pulling till A touches B

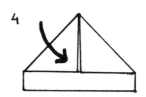

fold again and unfold

to make crease

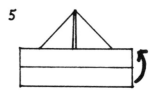

bring top fold down

along crease

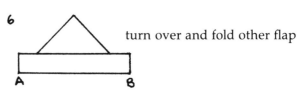

fold other side to match

fold one flap up

turn over and fold other flap

8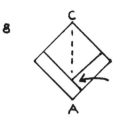

tuck one bottom flap
behind other

9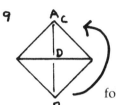

fold front up so A touches C

10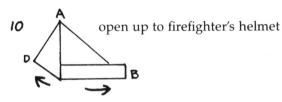

open up to firefighter's helmet

11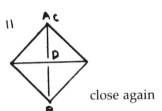

close again

12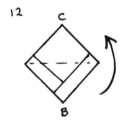

turn over, fold B up to C

13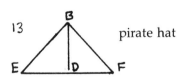

pirate hat

14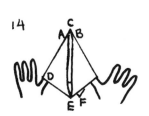

open pirate hat,
pull till E touches F

15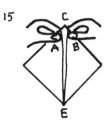

pinch A and B

16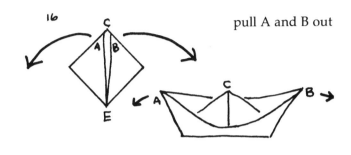

pull A and B out

17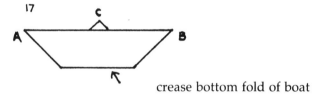

crease bottom fold of boat

18

tear off bow

19

turn boat around,
tear off stern

20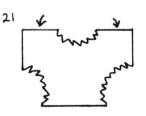

tear off peak, show hole,
lower boat

21

unfold to life jacket
(shoulders still folded),
raise jacket

THE HANDSOME PRINCE

ONCE UPON A TIME, a long time ago, in a land far away, there lived a king and a queen who had everything they wanted . . . except children. They waited, and they waited, and at last they had a son. He was a beautiful baby—so beautiful that they called him the Handsome Prince. The king and queen had no other children after that, and their son was so charming that they gave in to his every whim. So he grew from a beautiful baby, to a spoiled little boy, to an arrogant and self-indulgent young man who was always demanding his own way, and nearly always getting it. People still called him the Handsome Prince, but only out of habit, for he was so very lazy and self-indulgent that it showed in every line of his face and figure.

And so we have the Handsome Prince on the day when our story begins. It began like any other day in the prince's life—he woke up, opened one eye, and instantly his servants rushed to get his breakfast, which they brought to him on a tray carved of solid jade. They set the tray by his bedside, and the prince ate a bountiful breakfast in bed, as he always did. The instant he was finished, the servants whisked away the tray and brought him his shirt, which was made of the finest green silk (for green was the royal color of that kingdom). Then they brought him his pants, which were of exactly the same shade of green. The prince allowed his servants to dress him—he never dressed himself; he hardly knew how to button a button. Then he went downstairs to sit at a table all morning playing checkers with his courtiers. This was his favorite pastime, because they always let him win.

But this day was not to be like any other day in the prince's life, because on this day a soft spring breeze stole into the castle and lured the prince outside—out the gate, down the road, past the lazily turning windmills, and down to the river. It was the first time he had walked so far unattended.

When he got the river. the prince found the royal sailboat. He had never sailed it himself, but he thought that it, too, would obey his every whim, so he climbed in, untied it, and the boat went drifting down the river. At first the prince drifted past houses and barns and other boats of every description, but at last he came to a place where there were no barns, no houses, and his was the only boat on the river. And it was getting dark, and he was getting hungry. He tried to turn the boat around to make it go home, but he didn't know how. It was all he could do to get the boat to the riverbank and tie it up. He saw that there were no servants there to bring him his supper, and he realized that he would have to find someone who would.

He searched through the boat till he found a lantern, and managed to get it lit. Then he set off across the darkening countryside to see what he could find. At first he saw nothing but grass and sheep, but at last the rays of his lantern fell on a young woman, lying asleep under a tree. "A beautiful princess!" said the prince, for since she was beautiful, he assumed she must be a princess, though she was dressed like any shepherdess. "I will awaken her with a kiss!" But at that moment the young woman woke up. "You're not supposed to wake up until I kiss you," said the prince.

"What ever are you talking about?" said the young woman. "I wake up whenever I hear a sound, for I must protect my sheep."

"Well, I am going to kiss you anyway," said the prince, "because you are a beautiful girl and I am a handsome prince."

"But I don't want to kiss you! And as for handsome—with that soft white skin and that shiny green suit, you look just like a frog."

"A *frog*? Nonsense!" said the prince, and he kissed her anyway . . . and the moment he kissed her, he turned into a big, soft, green frog.

So, if you ever hear a story about a frog who was really a prince under an enchantment, now you know how he got that way.

The figures look best made from Japanese origami paper. It is square, colored on one side and white on the other. The largest size, about 8 inches square, is easiest to use. Typing paper, gift wrap, or any strong flexible paper may be cut square and used.

PRELIMINARY FOLDS:

1. Put paper flat on the table, colored side down.
2. Fold the square in half to a rectangle, crease.

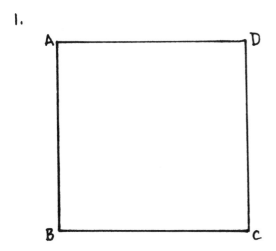

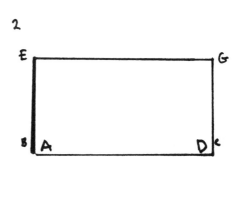

3. Fold the rectangle in half to a smaller square, crease.
4. Unfold the folds. Dotted lines show creases.

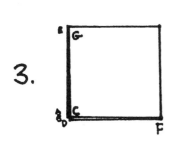

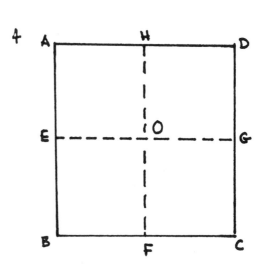

5. Fold corners A, B, C, and D to center O so edges of paper touch creased lines but do not overlap.
6. Turn figure over. Fold corners E, F, G, and H to center O. Do not overlap.
7. Turn figure over. Fold corners I, J, K, and L to center.

(Figures 8 on will be shown enlarged)

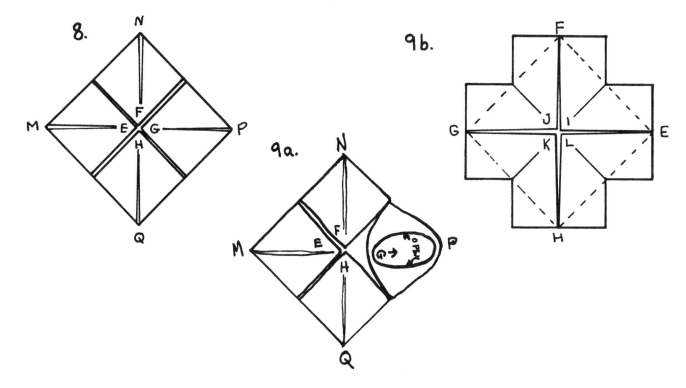

THE TRAY:

8. Turn figure 7 over.
9. Open out the four little squares (fig. 9a shows square G partly open) so that points E, F, G, and H each rest on corners M, N, P, and Q (fig. 9b), crease.

10. Turn over. Raise points I, J, K, and L to make four triangular legs to use as tray's stand.
11. Turn over.

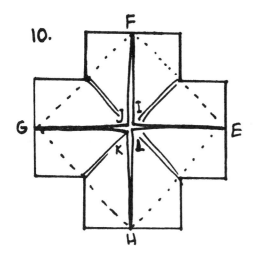

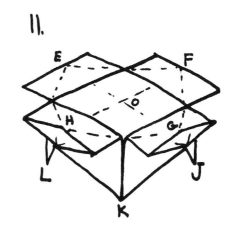

THE SHIRT:

12. Fold back the four legs (back to fig. 9b).
13. Fold fig. 9b in half (point F over point H).

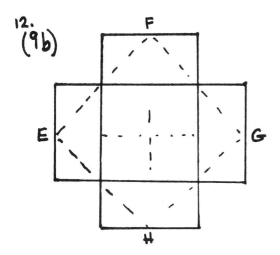

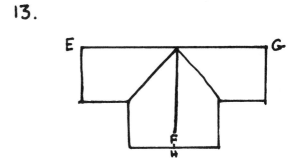

THE PANTS:

14. Unfold shirt back to fig. 9b. Unfold side flaps, bringing points E and G back to center O to reform small squares.

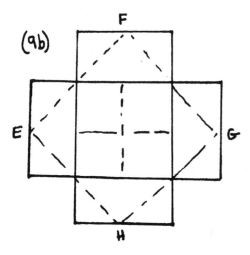

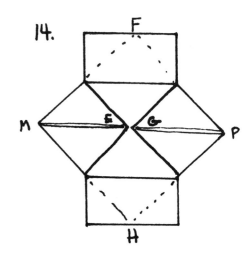

15. Turn figure over.
16. Unfold points I, J, K, and L.

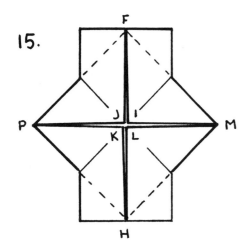

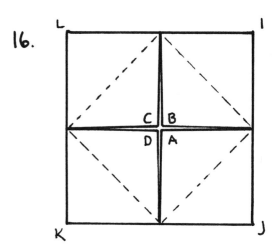

17. Turn figure over.
18. Unfold E and G.

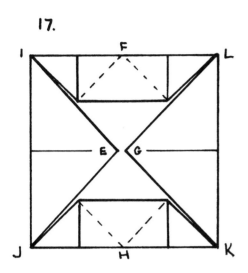

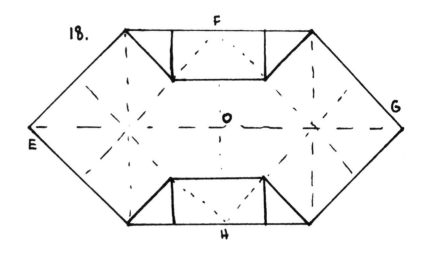

19. Turn over.
20. Fold points I, J, K, and L along the creases to center O leaving points E and G standing to form legs. Fold legs down.

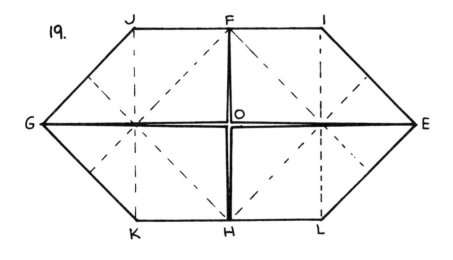

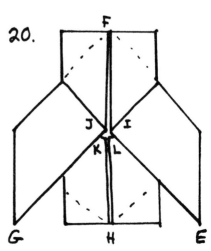

21. Turn figure over.
22. Fold H over on F along the creased line M-P.

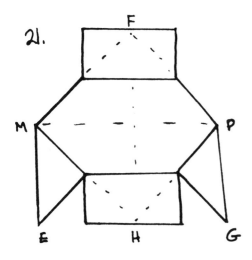

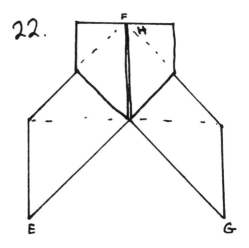

THE TABLE:

23. Unfold pants back to fig. 18.
24. Unfold F and H to center.

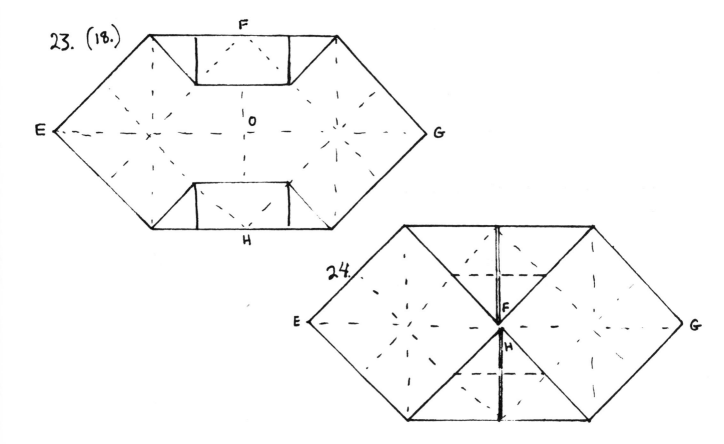

25. Unfold F and H away from center, turn figure over.
26. Bring points I, J, K, and L to the center, leaving corners E, F, G, and H standing to form four legs. Turn over.

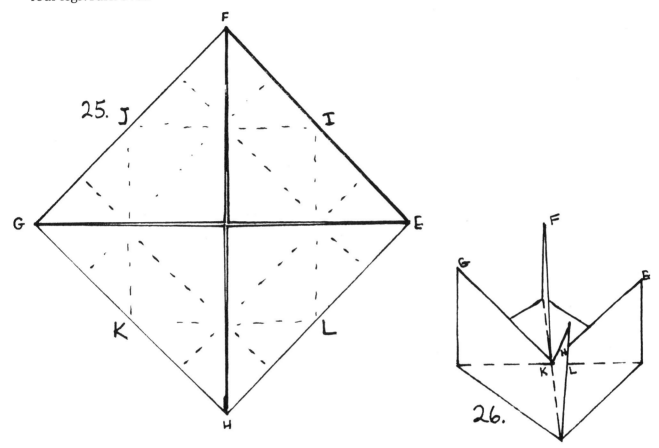

THE WINDMILL:

27. Start with fig. 26. Bend legs E, F, G, and H down clockwise.

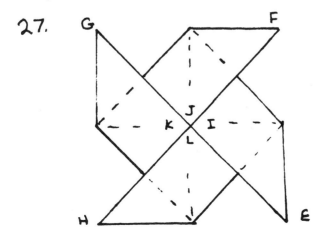

THE SAILBOAT:

28. Flip leg E to meet leg F. Flip leg H over, so that points G and H are on one line.
29. Turn over.

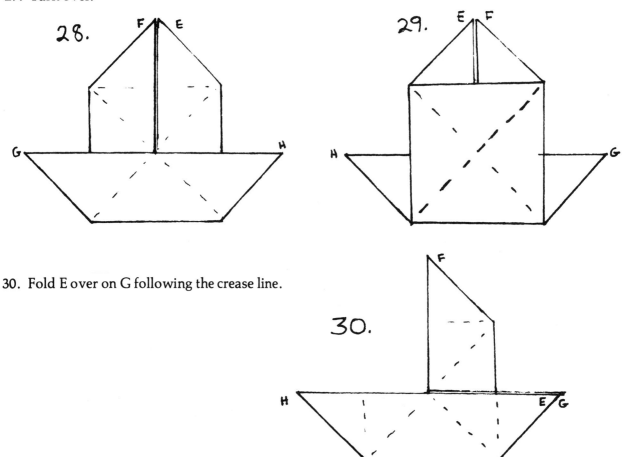

30. Fold E over on G following the crease line.

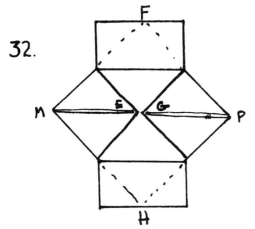

THE LANTERN:

31. Unfold the steps back to figure 25, then follow steps 6 through 8.
32. Open out squares F and H.

THE FROG:

33. Refold F to center.
34. Open out square E, so that two squares next to each other are open to form two eyes.
35. Turn over.

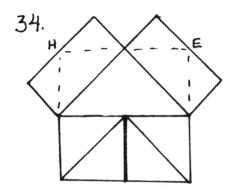

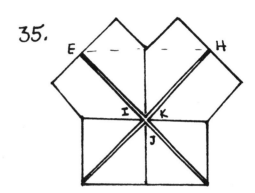

36. Unfold I, J, and K.
37. Turn over.

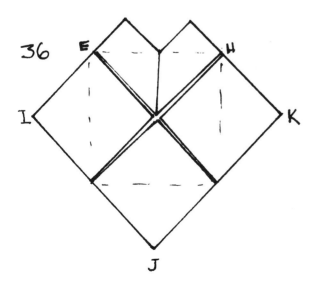

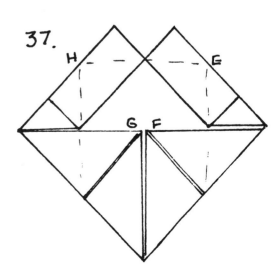

38. Unfold F and G.
39. Turn over. Bring points I, J, and K to center, leaving points F and G standing to form frog's hind legs. Lift flap L to form front of frog.

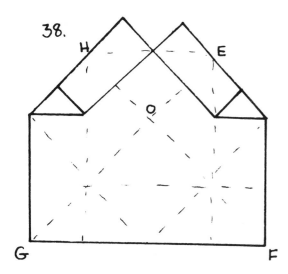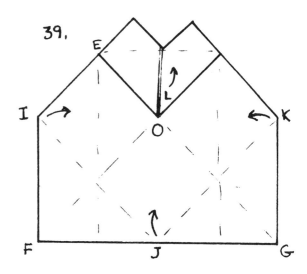

40. Turn over.

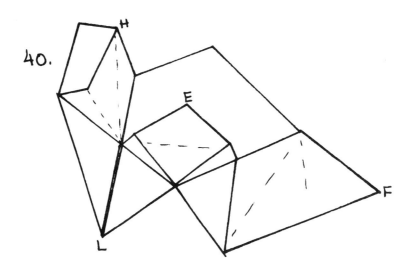

NOTE: If time is short, a group may be taught to make the frog directly from the tray (fig. 11) skipping the other figures. Holding the tray between flaps E and H, unfold the other two flaps so points F and G are returned to center O. Pull legs I, J, and K up and out level with the tray top. Unfold F and G to form fig. 38, continue as in 38 and 39 above. The front half of the frog is tray, the back half is table.

A STORY FOR HEATHER

ONCE THERE WAS a little girl named Heather. Every morning she drove the goats to pasture, through the valley and up the hillside to the meadow, and every evening she drove them home again. As she walked along behind the goats she always sang, songs she learned from her mother and father and songs she made up herself. In the morning she sang because she was happy and rested and ready for anything. In the evening she sang because a song is good company when you're alone with the goats and the shadows.

What Heather didn't know was that every day, as she walked through the valley, she walked right over a crossnore that lived under the ground—or rather I should say lived *in* the ground, for a crossnore moves through the earth like a shark through the sea or a tiger through the jungle. What they look like, nobody knows, for they never come out of the ground. This crossnore never moved far, though he wondered if the next valley might be better than his. He was always meaning to find out, but always wanting to get a good long sleep before he started, so *he* would be rested and ready for anything. And some meadowlark or thrush by day, some nightengale or melodious frog by night, was always waking him up in the middle of his good long sleep. Crossnores hate music. It always wakes them up, and the prettier the song, the more it wakes them up.

And the most annoying times in this crossnore's whole day were when he heard the trip-trap of the goats' hoofs (which he didn't mind at all) and the pad-pad-pad of little bare feet (which he didn't mind at all) and then Heather's high, clear voice singing some beautiful song (which he minded awfully). He longed to grab Heather by her little bare toes and drag her into the ground and stop up her mouth with dirt, but her voice was so clear and sweet that he coudn't bear to get near enough to do it. So he bided his time, and grumbled.

Then, one day, the goats passed overhead, and the pad-pad-pad of little bare feet, but the crossnore did not hear any singing. Heather had a cold and could not sing a note. In the morning, the crossnore was too surprised to catch her, but all day long, as he muttered at thrushes and shouldered sharp stones out of his bed, he plotted and planned to grab Heather's little bare toes and drag her under the ground that very night.

And all day long Heather thought how lonesome it would be, walking home through the evening shadows without a song for company. In the evening, when she started down the path, she still couldn't sing. At the head of the valley, she passed a clump of willows. She took out her knife and snicked off a piece of willow as she went by, and started to whittle as she walked. And as she walked, the crossnore waited, and listened, and soon he heard the trip-trap of the goats' hoofs, and the pad-pad-pad of Heather's little bare feet, but just as he grabbed for her little bare toes, she raised her new-made willow whistle to her lips and blew the clearest, sweetest tune the crossnore had ever heard. He dove straight down into the earth so fast the ground sank three feet right under Heather, and Heather sank with it. She climbed out of the hole and whistled her way home, and the crossnore moved to the next valley and never came back.

When Heather got home, she told her mother and father what had happened to her. They told her a nice story about underground streams and sinkholes, and she almost believed it, but she won't know what really happened until she hears the story of How Heather Whistled Away the Crossnore.

THE PANCAKE

C: *One morning, a goodwife was cooking a sweet milk pancake over the fire. The pancake lay in the pan, frizzling away, so beautiful and thick, it was a pleasure to look at. The children were standing 'round the fire, and the goodman sat in the corner and looked on. The pancake smelled so good that the children started begging for a bite.*

P: Please, mother, give me a bite of pancake, *said one.*

C: Please, dear mother, give me a bite of pancake, *said the second.*

P: Please, dear, good mother, give me a bite of pancake, *said the third.*

C: Please, dear, good, kind mother, give me a bite of pancake, *said the fourth.*

P: Please, dear, good, kind, sweet mother, give me a bite of pancake, *said the fifth.*

C: Please, dear, good, kind, sweet, generous mother, give me a bite of pancake, *said the fifth.*

P: Please, dear, good, kind, sweet, generous, clever mother, give me a bite of pancake, *said the seventh.*

C: *And each one begged more prettily than the other, for they were so hungry,*

P: *and they were such good children.*

C: Yes, **dears,** *said their mother,* but it is not done yet. You must wait until it turns itself.

P: *Now, she should not have said 'wait until it turns itself,'*

C: *she should have said 'wait until I turn the pancake,' for the pancake lay in the pan and thought,*

P: must I turn myself?

C: *And the pancake tried to turn itself*

P: *but it was too soft.*

C: *So it waited until it had cooked a bit longer, and was firmer in the flesh, and then it tried again*

P: *and it turned itself right over.*

C: *And when it had cooked a while on the other side, and was all golden brown, it was so strong*

P: *that it jumped right out of the pan and started rolling across the floor like a wheel.*

C: Stop, pancake! *cried the goodwife, running after it.*

P: *But the pancake rolled right out the door.*

C: Stop, pancake! *cried the goodman, running after the goodwife,*

P: *but the pancake rolled down the path and out the gate.*

C: Stop, pancake! *cried the seven hungry children, running after the goodman,*

P: *but the pancake rolled down the road and soon left them all far behind.*

C: *After a while,*

P: *the pancake met a hen.*

C: Good morning, pancake, *said the hen.*

P: Good morning, Henny Penny, *said the pancake, and kept rolling.*

C: Pancake, dear, don't roll so fast! Bide a bit and let me eat you.

P: Oh, no! I ran away from the goodwife and her goodman and their seven squalling children and I shall run away from you too, Henny Penny.

C: *The pancake rolled on*

P: *until it met a duck.*

C: Good morning, pancake.

P: Good morning, Ducky Lucky, *said the pancake, and kept rolling.*

C: Pancake, dear, don't roll so fast. Bide a bit and let me eat you.

P: Oh, no! I ran away from the goodwife and her goodman and their seven squalling children and Henny Penny, and I shall run away from you too, Ducky Lucky.

C: *The pancake rolled on*

P: *until it met a goose.*

C: Good morning, pancake.

P: Good morning, Goosey Loosey, *said the pancake, and kept rolling.*

C: Pancake, dear, don't roll so fast. Bide a bit and let me eat you.

P: Oh, no! I ran away from the goodwife and her goodman and their seven squalling children and Henny Penny and Ducky Lucky, and I shall run away from you too, Goosey Loosey.

C: *And the pancake rolled on*

P: *until it came to a pig.*

C: Good morning, pancake.

P: Good morning, Piggy Wiggy, *said the pancake, and rolled faster than ever.*

C: Nay, wait a bit, you needn't be in such a hurry. I see you are coming to the woods, and they say it isn't very safe there. We two should travel together, and keep each other company.

P: Well, there may be something in that. *So the pancake slowed down,*

C: *and the pig trotted up,*

P & C: *and side by side they entered the woods, and side by side they went along*

P: *until they came to a stream.*

C: *The pig was nice and fat and could swim very well, but the pancake said,*

P: How am I to get across? I cannot swim at all.

C: Hop on my snout, and I'll carry you across.

P: *The pancake did so.*

C: *And the pig carried it to the middle of the stream, and then, Ouf! Ouf! he tossed the pancake in the air, caught it in his mouth, and swallowed it in one gulp.*

P: *And as the pancake could not go any farther,*

C: *the story can't go any farther either.*

Children's Lore

CHILDREN HAVE THEIR OWN FOLKLORE—counting-out rhymes, skip-rope rhymes, taunts and singing games—which they have handed down for hundreds of years without adult assistance. "The games are a form of lore, a tradition which in certain aspects reaches back into tribal origins . . . we adults—teachers especially—watching children at their games, tend to think that because children are new, we ourselves have a great deal to offer. We neglect to observe that we are competing with a durable and compelling tradition."*

It might make sense for children to begin their study of folklore with their own lore, rather than with the stories of Paul Bunyan or Pecos Bill (for a folklorist's view of the Paul Bunyan tales, see Richard Dorson's informative and entertaining *America in Legend, Folklore from the Colonial Period to the Present,* Pantheon, 1973, pp. 168–170).

Shimmy Shimmy Coke-Ca-Pop: A Collection of City Children's Street Games and Rhymes by John and Carol Langstaff (Doubleday, 1973), *1, 2, 3 and a Zing Zing*

---

*Dennison, George. *The Lives of Children: The Story of the First Street School.* Random, 1970. p. 202.

Zing, collected by Tony Schwartz (Folkways Records FC 7003) and other collections of children's lore can be used, not to teach the games and rhymes to children, who already know them, but to draw their attention to local variations, so they will begin to grasp the notion that there are many "right" versions of folklore. It should then be easier for them to accept versions of folktales different from the ones they are used to. They may even be inspired to make their own collection by taping or writing down the rhymes they know, and asking friends, parents, teachers for their versions.

And to deepen our own appreciation of this rich tradition which surrounds those of us who work with children, there are several excellent studies of the history, meaning and function of the games and rhymes:

Jones, Bessie, and Bess Lomax Hawes. *Step It Down: Games, Plays, Songs, and Stories from the Afro-American Heritage.* Harper, 1972.

Knapp, Mary and Herbert. *One Potato, Two Potato . . . The Secret Education of American Children.* Norton, 1976.

Opie, Iona and Peter. *The Lore and Language of School-children.* Clarendon Press, 1959.

Using Stories, in Programs and Out

MOST STORYTELLING is not done in story programs. Speakers and teachers illustrate points and enliven talks with stories, singers introduce songs with stories, parents put children to sleep with stories. Leo Rosten, in his introduction to his dictionary, *The Joys of Yiddish*, says:

"I have used a story, joke, or anecdote in the main body of this lexicon to illustrate the meaning of a word, whenever possible. Since this is highly unorthodox in lexicography, a brief for the defense may be in order.

"I consider the story, the anecdote, the joke, a teaching instrument of unique efficacy. A joke is a structured, compact narrative that makes a point with power, generally by surprise. A good story is exceedingly hard for anyone to forget. It is therefore an excellent pedagogic peg on which to hang a point. Those who do not use stories when they try to explain or communicate are either inept at telling them or blindly forfeit a tool of great utility."

Librarians and teachers need not restrict their use of storytelling to story-time. Librarians can use stories in class visits where their primary purpose is book talks or library instruction, and in talks to teachers, community organizations, et cetera, to break the ice, make a point, encourage storytelling, or promote support of library programs.

Teachers can use stories to introduce new topics, fill waiting time, and give examples of conflicts similar to ones arising in class, which may encourage discussion of things otherwise hard to talk about calmly.

Folktales and folklore can be used to explore cultural differences and similarities. In "Culture's Storehouse: Building Humanities Skills Through Folklore" (*Intercom*, Dec. 1978, entire double issue), Judith M. Barnet presents a whole language arts and social studies unit for secondary schools based on folktales, proverbs and folk games, with excellent suggestions for activities and discussion. Some of the ideas would work well in upper elementary grades.

Stories can be told almost anywhere, under almost any circumstances, though I have found that doing a story program in competition with a nearby bagpiper is a losing battle. At an outdoor, shopping mall, or festival setting, it is good to have a friend or assistant to steer wandering musicians or loud conversations elsewhere. Another storyteller, who can protect you and spell you off as well, is even more useful, as it is usually easier to keep a crowd than to attract one, in these circumstances.

Ideally, I like to be in a fairly quiet but not silent place, with a barrier behind me so that the audience is not distracted by passers-by, but with no barrier defining the limits of the audience area, so people feel free to come and go, and listen while pretending not to. Indoors or out, I try to be facing the light source, so my audience is not squinting into it. Whether I stand, perch on a table or stool, sit in a chair, or sit on the floor depends on the size, age and formality of the group, but I try to place myself so everybody can see me, and vice versa, without removing myself too far from the audience. If there are chairs for the audience, I feel best when they are in about third-of-a-circle curves—more informal than straight lines, but not so hard for me to look at as a half-circle or whole circle.

Circumstances, of course, are rarely ideal. I try to think ahead to avert interruptions—is there someone to answer the phone? can we disconnect the intercom announcement system? ask the clerk to schedule typing for other than storytimes? But the best insurance is to know the story well enough to be able to stop, wait for the fire engines to go by, and pick up the thread again without getting lost.

What about interruptions from young audiences? Some of them can be prevented by saying in your introduction, "If you know this story, just smile, and I'll know you know, but let's keep the ending a secret between us." If the interruption is a question related to the story that can be answered very briefly, I do so. Other questions and comments I try to acknowledge but not answer. It's no use trying to ignore them; the child will just think you didn't hear and will repeat the comment louder. Nod, or say "That's nice," or "I'll tell you later," and go on. Then pick up on it again when the story is over. An assistant can help here, too, to take care of needs that can't wait.

Pre-school story-time is a special challenge, since many pre-schoolers are not used to listening, or even being, in groups , no matter how well they listen individually at home. For this reason, many libraries restrict storytimes to three-year-olds and older. Storytimes for children younger than three can work if the children are on on parents' laps. Stretches, songs, fingerplays, Mother Goose rhymes and conversation can help sustain attention during a program for young children. You can remove a major distraction by asking the children to give you the books they are looking at and any toys they brought, so you can put them on a table in front, to be claimed later. Some kind of ritual, such as beginning with the same song or fingerplay each week, or lighting a storytime candle, serves as a signal that it's time to listen and also provides the security of the familiar. Children like favorite stories repeated from time to time also. It helps to keep a list of what you've done. *Pre-School Story Hour* by Vardine Moore (Scarecrow, 1972) has good story suggestions and techniques for this age.

For any age, I like to have a theme for the program. A theme enables me to go from one story to the next in a simple, conversational way, and helps me remember what I'm doing next, but it is not necessary and I don't always have one. I don't generally announce the title of a story before I tell it, especially if the title gives away something better disclosed in the course of the story. I try to remember to give some idea of what's coming up when I begin the program, and to start with a short story so newcomers to story programs will have an idea of what a story is like and a sense of completion right away. Then I might tell a longer story, perhaps one that requires concentration from the listener. Then a stretch, song, or short story for a change of pace, and end with a story that is an attention-keeper, either through suspense, humor, or audience participation. This is not a rule, and will certainly need to be varied at times. If the attention-keeper has a violent ending, or a sad one, it might go better in the middle of the program, or be followed at the end by a short, comforting story or song.

I usually warn the audience if I am going to tell a scary or bloody story; then they can brace themselves, and say "That wasn't so scary" afterwards. And it wasn't so scary, listening in a group, but it might be, thinking about it alone later. Kathryn Windham, who tells ghost stories most convincingly, also passes on a few beliefs about how to keep ghosts away at night; the simplest being to place your shoes with one pointing toward your bed and one pointing away.

People tend to remember liking certain stories at a younger age than they actually did, and consequently try myths, fairy tales, and *Alice in Wonderland* on children too young for them. According to Josephine Gardner, whose little Porpoise Press pamphlet, *How to Tell a Story,* is long out of print, "Children under the age of five years do not need fairy tales. The world is sufficiently wonderful to them." I think some of the objection to violence in fairy tales is a result of assuming that they are for very young children, which they are not. The more complicated fairy tales require an audience much older than five, as do the myths, whose power and strangeness is lost in simplified versions intended for younger children.

Some stories appeal to a wide age range, and come in handy when a teller is faced with a mixed audience of pre-school and older children. I use "The Foolish Frog," "Lazy Jack," "The Lion in the Path," "The Rainhat," and "Habit."

How long should a program be? The youngest and very oldest prefer short programs of short stories; older children I usually tell to for about forty-five minutes; my adult programs are generally one and one-half hours with a break. I start preschoolers at about twenty minutes, lengthening this to around thirty-five minutes as they get used to listening, become familiar with the songs, and as we get to talking together between stories.

Listeners in convalescent homes, aged and infirm, need programs planned especially for them. They are often physically uncomfortable or straining to hear, so each story should be short, none more than eight minutes. An old familiar tale will reach those who remember but have trouble understanding something new. A story of human foibles or cleverness will amuse those whose infirmities are physical, not mental. A list of stories recommended for adult audiences follows this chapter. As the old are often treated as children and understandably resent this, it is better to start with stories clearly meant for adults, and wait till rapport is established before telling stories that might be perceived as "kid stuff." Telling in rest homes requires commitment on the part of the teller. If you visit once or twice and then stop, you could be one more disappointment to people who may already feel abandoned. The teller also needs the cooperation of those running the home, as an attendant's presence is often necessary when telling to groups. A sound system and visual aids with stories will help you reach those who have difficulty hearing. Not all the residents will be able to express their appreciation of live entertainment as a relief from constant television; but those who can, make this rather difficult storytelling situation one of the most rewarding ones. And for the teller interested in oral history, the old are a valuable source of stories.

As a storyteller, you may or may not be involved in publicizing story programs. If you are, you can find many ideas in Bauer's *Handbook for Storytellers*. If this essential is neglected, your other preparations may be for naught, so it is best to be aware of what publicity is being done for your program.

People sometimes suggest that storytellers wear dangling jewelry or bright colors or fancy hats to attract and keep the attention of the audience. I would rather let the story attract and hold the audience if it can, and dress for physical comfort and for the mental comfort of knowing that I am dressed appropriately for the occasion. I have told stories in full costume at a Renaissance Faire, barefoot at a picnic, in a proper dress at a convalescent hospital, in jeans at a nursery school, in a long dress on stage, but I usually wear for storytelling what I usually wear for any public occasion. I happen to like bright colors sometimes, but I don't like hats or flashy jewelry, so I don't wear them. I know people don't have to be looking at me in order to listen, and I want them to remember what they heard, not what I wore.

After the stories, the publicity, the staff, and the location are prepared, there is one last thing to do: prepare yourself. If you can possibly arrange it, take a few minutes by yourself before you start the program to go over the order of the stories in your mind, and make sure everything is set up. Wiggle your shoulders, swing your arms, roll your head around, make some faces. Then close your eyes, take a deep breath, and relax. You're on.

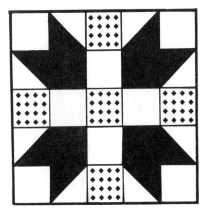

I never met a storyteller who doubted the value of his or her efforts. We all know in our bones that enjoyment of stories motivates kids to read. And we are not surprised when we read Tim Jennings' account[1] of winning the attention of a group of twelve-year-old nonreaders by telling folktales, when all his attempts to get them to listen to him read stories aloud had failed. But sometimes we need to convince others, if storytelling is to be budgeted, or even allowed. A recent survey of California libraries by Robert Grover and Mary Kevin Moore shows that only 19.7% of public libraries offer regular (weekly or monthly) story hours for older children, while 62.2% offer regular pre-school story hours (which take less staff time to prepare, as the stories are usually read, not told). 39.7% offer regular film programs.[2]

There have been few studies of the effects of telling, and fewer rigorous ones with clear results that would convince library and school boards of the worth of story programs. A study by Anthony Amato, Elsie Ziegler and Robert Evans, reported in 1973, showed no measurable effects of either storytelling or creative dramatics on reading interest or ability, though the group attending storytelling did increase scores on a test of creativity.[3]

In 1977, Garth H. Brown studied the relation of a child's "sense of story" (the sense of how a story should progress logically, which helps the child predict *what* is likely to be stated on the printed page and *how* it might be written) to the child's reading ability, and concluded: "The inability to develop reading much beyond a plodding and tedious almost word by word performance, appears related to difficulty in 'moving into' the language of story. . . . It may be true, too, that the *extent* of the child's sense of story influences comprehension [comprehension being defined as the ability to retell a story read]. . . . Listening to stories being told or read aloud throughout the elementary school must be helpful and seems crucial to reading and writing growth."[4]

To test the helpfulness of storytelling in developing comprehension, Catherine Farrell studied the effects of storytelling by teachers and professional storytellers in two kindergartens and two first grades in 1981–1982. Students who heard many stories during the school year showed more improvement in their ability to retell a story they heard, and to make up original story elements to extend the story, than did students in the control classes not exposed to storytelling.[5]

1. Jennings, Tim. "Storytelling—A Nonliterate Approach to Reading," *Learning Magazine* April/May 1981, pp. 48–52. Reprinted in *The Yarnspinner* Nov. 1981.

2. Grover, Robert, and Mary Kevin Moore. "Print Dominates Library Service to Children," *American Libraries* April 1982, pp. 268–9.

3. Amato, Anthony, et al. "The Effectiveness of Creative Dramatics and Storytelling in a Library Setting," *The Journal of Educational Research* Dec. 1973, pp. 161 + .

4. Brown, Garth H. "Development of Story in Children's Reading and Writing," *Theory into Practice* Dec. 1977, pp. 357–361.

5. Farrell, Catherine Horne. *Word Weaving Study Report.* To be available from Word Weaving, P.O. Box 5646, San Francisco, CA 94101.

SOURCES FOR STORIES TO TELL TO ADULTS

MANY STORIES WRITTEN FOR ADULTS are too complex to tell, but many stories written or retold for children are of interest to adults. Here are some books published for children and adults which contain stories appropriate to adult audiences from senior high schools to senior centers. Some stories particularly suited to junior high are indicated by bold face.

Anderson, Hans. *It's Perfectly True and Other Stories.* Translated by Paul Leyssac. Harcourt, 1938.

Arabian Nights. Collected and edited by Andrew Lang. David McKay, 1946.

Ashabranner, Brent, and Russell Davis. *The Lion's Whiskers, Tales of High Africa.* Little, Brown, 1959.

Babbitt, Natalie. *The Devil's Storybook.* Farrar, 1974. Especially "Perfection" and **"The Power of Speech."**

Bang, Garrett. *Men from the Village Deep in the Mountains.* Macmillan, 1973. "Patches."

Berson, Harold. *How the Devil Gets His Due.* Crown, 1972.

Chase, Richard. *American Folk Tales and Songs.* Dover reprint. Especially "Pack Down the Big Chest" and **"Seven Irishmen"** (which can—and should—be told as "Seven Brothers.")

— *Grandfather Tales.* Houghton, 1948. Especially **"Wicked John and the Devil"** and **"Old Dry Frye."**

Clemens, Samuel. *The Complete Short Stories of Mark Twain.* Especially "The Notorious Jumping Frog of Calaveras County."

Courlander, Harold, and George Herzog. *The Cow Tail Switch and Other West African Stories.* Holt, 1947. Especially the title story and **"Talk."**

—. *The Piece of Fire and Other Haitian Tales.* Harcourt, 1964. Especially **"Ticoumba and the President."**

—. *The Tiger's Whisker, and Other Tales from Asia and the Pacific.* Harcourt, 1959. Especially "The Scholars and the Lion."

Davenport, Basil. *Tales to Be Told in the Dark.* Dodd, 1953. Especially "The Mujina" ("Two Anecdotes," p. 245). "The Mujina" is also in Laughton's *Tell Me a Story.*

Dobie, J. Frank. *Legends of Texas,* Vols. I and II. Pelican, 1975.

Evslin, Bernard. *The Green Hero; Early Adventures of Fin McCool.* Four Winds, 1975.

Family Folklore. Pantheon, 1982 (1976).

Farjeon, Eleanor. *The Little Bookroom.* Oxford University Press, 1956. Especially "The Seventh Princess."

—. *Martin Pippin in the Daisy Field.* Stokes, 1938. "Elsie Piddock Skips in Her Sleep." Reprinted in Eileen Colwell's *A Storyteller's Choice,* Walck, 1964.

Feinberg, Karen. *The Star in the Apple.* Gloria Mundi Press (forthcoming).

Galdone, Paul. *The Wise Fool.* Random, 1968. Based on a tale from *The Third Book of Pantagruel* by Rabelais.

Ginsburg, Mirra. *The Lazies, Tales of the Peoples of Russia.* Macmillan, 1973. Especially **"Sheidulla"** and "Two Frogs."

Henry, O. *Best Short Stories of O. Henry.* Doubleday, 1965. Especially "The Gift of the Magi."

Housman, Laurence. *The Rat Catcher's Daughter.* Atheneum, 1974.

Howe, Irving, and Ilana Wiener Howe. *Short Shorts.* Godine, 1982.

Jacobs, Joseph. *English Fairy Tales.* Putnam, 1898. Especially **"Mr. Fox"** and "Master of All Masters."

—. *More English Fairy Tales.* Putnam, 1904. Especially "The Pedlar of Swaffham."

Kelsey, Alice. *Once the Hodja.* Longmans, 1943.

—. *Once the Mullah.* Longmans, 1954.

Kennedy, Richard. *Come Again in the Spring.* Harper, 1976.

—. *Crazy in Love.* Dutton, 1980.

—. *The Porcelain Man.* Little, 1976.

Kipling, Rudyard. *Just So Stories.* Doubleday, 1912. Especially "The Cat That Walked by Himself."

Kroeber, Theodora. *The Inland Whale: Nine Stories Retold from California Indian Legends.* University of California Press, 1959.

Langner, Nola. *Go and Shut the Door.* Dial, 1971.

Laughton, Charles. *Tell Me a Story.* McGraw-Hill, 1957.

Lobel, Arnold. *Fables.* Harper, 1980.

Longfellow, Henry W. *Paul Revere's Ride.* Crowell, 1963.

Minard, Rosemary. *Womenfolk and Fairy Tales.* Houghton, 1975.

Phelps, Ethel Johnston. *The Maid of the North: Feminist Folk Tales from Around the World.* Holt, 1981.

Pinkwater, Manus. *Wizard Crystal.* Dodd, 1973.

Ritchie, Alice. *Treasure of Li-Po.* Harcourt, 1949. **"Two of Everything."**

Sandburg, Carl. *The Rootabaga Stories.* Harcourt, 1922. Especially "The White Horse Girl and the Blue Wind Boy."

Schimmel, Nancy. *Just Enough to Make a Story.* Sisters' Choice, 1978, 1982. **"The Rainhat"** and **"The Handsome Prince."**

—. *Plum Pudding.* Sisters' Choice Records. "The Woodcutter's Story."

Service, Robert. *The Shooting of Dan McGrew. The Cremation of Sam McGee.* Young Scott, 1969.

Serwer, Blanche. *Let's Steal the Moon: Jewish Tales, Ancient and Recent.* Little, Brown, 1970. Especially "Did the Tailor Have a Nightmare?"

Shah, Idries. *Tales of the Dervishes.* Dutton, 1970.

—. *World Tales.* Harcourt, 1979.

Singer, Isaac B. *The Fearsome Inn.* Scribner, 1967.

Stockton, Frank. *The Storyteller's Pack.* Scribner, 1968. "The Lady or the Tiger?"

Tashjian, Virginia. *Once There Was and Was Not; Armenian Tales Retold.* Little, Brown, 1966.

—. *Juba This and Juba That: Story Hour Stretches for Large or Small Groups.* Little, Brown, 1966. **"The Yellow Ribbon."**

Thurber, James. *Fables for Our Time.* Harper, 1952.

Troughton, Joanna. *Sir Gawain and the Loathly Damsel.* Dutton, 1972.

Van der Post, Laurens. *Patterns of Renewal.* Pendle Hill, 1962. Especially pp. 4 and 5 for the story about the basket.

Viorst, Judith. *Alexander and the Terrible, Horrible, No Good, Very Bad Day.* Atheneum, 1972.

Williams, Jay. *Petronella.* Parents' Magazine Press, o.p.

—. *The Practical Princess and Other Liberating Fairy Tales.* Four Winds, 1978, Scholastic. (Includes "Petronella.")

Wolkstein, Diane. *The Magic Orange Tree and Other Haitian Folktales.* Knopf, 1978. Especially "Owl."

Yolen, Jane. *Dream Weaver.* Philomel, 1979. Especially **"The Cat Bride."**

—. *The Moon Ribbon and Other Tales.* Crowell, 1976. Especially "Somewhen."

Zemach, Harve. *A Penny a Look: An Old Story Retold.* Farrar, 1971.

This list was developed from one compiled by Susan Patron and Nancy Schimmel for THAT REMINDS ME OF A STORY, a seminar on the uses of storytelling with older people presented at the Craft and Folk Arts Museum in cooperation with the Los Angeles Public Library, and partially funded by the National Endowment for the Arts. It may be reproduced without permission (if credit is given) by any library, school, or other non-profit institution.

Active Heroines in Folktales for Children

In most familiar folk tales with female protaganists, the woman or girl plays a passive role, waiting to be rescued or, at most, helping her rescuer by her special knowledge of her captor. Women with power tend to have secondary roles: wicked stepmother, fairy godmother. Some folk tales in which the central female character takes an active, positive role are listed here. In two of the stories, "Umai" and "The Wood Maiden" ("The Wood Fairy"), there are no male characters.

In this index to unusual women in traditional stories found in collections for children, the annotations are mostly descriptive. Political or literary analysis is left to you, as is selection of stories which you feel are both non-sexist and good for telling.

Since this list was first compiled, several books of folk tales with active heroines have been published. Stories from the first, *Womenfolk and Fairy Tales*, are annotated here. Two books by Ethel Johnston Phelps, *Tatterhood and Other Tales* (Feminist Press, 1978) and *The Maid of the North, Feminist Folk Tales from Around the World* (Holt, 1981), and one by Toni McCarty, *The Skull in the Snow* (Delacorte, 1981), are also essential to the feminist storyteller. Phelps does more cleaning up of sexist tales than I am comfortable with—I want the tales I tell to represent a *tradition* of uppity women. I will change sexist language, but not plots or characters.

If you know of other stories in folk tale collections for children that seem to belong on this list, please send a description and source for the stories to Sisters' Choice, 2027 Parker Street, Berkeley, CA 94704.

Story titles marked with an asterisk (*) are also the book title. A source list follows the story list.

Atalanta
from *Free to Be . . . You and Me*.
A modern retelling of the myth, in which Atalanta and Young John tie in the race and become friends. Also many traditional versions in which the young man wins the race and Atalanta by cleverness, as Atalanta is still the best runner.

Baba Yaga
from *Old Peter's Russian Tales*.
The little girl sent to the witch's house uses thoughtfully everything she finds, and thus makes her escape.

The Barber's Clever Wife
from *Tales from the Punjab, Fools and Funny Fellows*.
She dupes a pack of thieves on four occasions and finally bites off the tip of their captain's tongue.

The Beggar in the Blanket*
A woman's audacious plan convinces her husband that his poor brother is worth more to him than his rich friends.

The Betrothal Gifts
from *Czechoslovak Fairy Tales*.
A young man takes as his fiancée a frog whose gifts outshine those of his brothers' fiancées, winning him his father's wealth and thereby breaking her enchantment.

The Black Bull of Norroway
from *More English Folk and Fairy Tales*.
Three sisters go out to seek their fortunes; the third rides the black bull and rescues her true love from an evil spell.

Boadicea . . . The Warrior Queen
from *The World's Great Stories*.
The legend of England's heroine.

Cap o' Rushes*
also in *English Folk and Fairy Tales, Favorite Fairy Tales Told in England, Womenfolk and Fairy Tales.*
The youngest daughter is disowned because her father dislikes her plain reply to his question, "How much do you love me?" She makes her own way, marries, and convinces her father he was wrong.

Chinese Red Riding Hoods
from *Chinese Fairy Tales.*
The eldest daughter is not fooled by the wolf in grandma's clothing, and the three girls kill him.

Clever Carmelita
from *South American Wonder Tales.*
The clever governor of a Chilean town chooses a wife who can top all his jokes, but when she exposes his dishonesty in a way that makes *him* a joke, she has to figure her way out of a death sentence.

Clever Grethel
from *Tales Told Again, Clever Cooks, Womenfolk and Fairy Tales, Household Stories.*
The cook succumbs to temptation and eats the dinner, then tricks both her master and his guest to throw the blame off herself.

Clever Kadra
from *African Wonder Tales.*
A young woman outwits and marries the willful ruler of Cairo.

Clever Manka
from *The Shepherd's Nosegay, Time for Fairy Tales, Fools and Funny Fellows, Womenfolk and Fairy Tales.*
Manka solves the burgomaster's riddles, marries him, disobeys his order not to show herself more clever than he, and outwits him again in order to keep him.

Clever Oonagh
from *William Mayne's Book of Giants, Clever Cooks.*
Fin is afraid to fight Cucullin, a bigger giant, so Fin's wife tricks Cucullin.

The Clever Peasant Girl
from *The Moon Painters.*
A story similar to "Clever Manka": different riddles, same ending.

Davit
from *Yes and No Stories.*
Svetlana journeys to the sun to find a cure for her brother, and aided by the sun's mother, solves the problems of the woman in labor, the sheep and the stag as well. Georgian Russian.

The Dragon's Revenge
from *Magic Animals of Japan.*
A young man breaks his promise to the woman who loves him; she turns into a dragon and burns him to a crisp.

East of the Sun and West of the Moon*
also in *True and Untrue, Womenfolk and Fairy Tales.*
A woman whose husband vanishes under an enchantment goes on a long and dangerous journey to free him.

The Feather of Finist the Falcon
from *Russian Wonder Tales.*
Similar to "East of the Sun and West of the Moon."

Fin M'Coul and Cucullin
from *A Book of Giants.*
A shorter and less humorous telling of "Clever Oonagh."

The Foot Racers of Payupki
from *People of the Short Blue Corn.*
The men of Tikuvi reject Spider Grandmother's protection for their runners, so she goes to Payupki, where the men welcome her. Payupki's runner wins, but as he trains for the challenge race, he discovers that his sister runs faster than he. The Tikuvi men use sorcery against the girl, but with Spider Grandmother's protection, she wins.

The Forty Thieves
from *The Blue Fairy Book, Womenfolk and Fairy Tales.*
Morgiana, the wise slave, saves Ali Baba from the thieves and marries his son.

A Fox Who Was Too Sly
from *Magic Animals of Japan.*
The fox tries to trick an old woman but she tricks—and cooks—him.

The Gay Goss-hawk
from *Heather and Broom.*
An English lady, prevented by her father from marrying her Scottish laird, carries out a bold plan to join her true love. Retold from a ballad.

The Girl Who Overpowered the Moon
from *The Man in the Moon*.
A Siberian (Chukchee) tale in which a reindeer herder is pursued by the moon. She keeps tricking the moon until he is exhausted and promises to give her people light at night and to measure the year for them.

The Goblin's Giggle*
A bride stolen away by goblins is rescued by her mother and a nun. When the goblins drink the river to catch them, they escape by making the goblins laugh.

The Golden Shoe
from *Scandinavian Stories*.
Kari and her horse, Sleipnir, escape from her wicked stepmother and Kari becomes a servant in the house of a young chieftain. He insults her, but when she appears in church in the elegant clothing Sleipnir provides, the chieftain, not recognizing her, says he will marry the maiden who fits the golden shoe Kari has left behind. She tries on the shoe, rejects him, and rides off on Sleipnir, who turns into a handsome young farmer. Iceland.

Half a Kingdom*
A poor peasant rescues the prince from trolls, wins half the kingdom, and, after thinking it over, agrees to marry the prince. Iceland.

The Husband Who Was to Mind the House
from *East of the Sun and West of the Moon, Time for Fairy Tales, True and Untrue*.
A farmer finds that his wife's work is not so easy as he thinks.

I'm Tipingee, She's Tipingee, We're Tipingee, Too
from *The Magic Orange Tree*.
Tipingee organizes her friends to keep the old man from taking her away.

Kate Crackernuts
from *English Folk & Fairy Tales, Womenfolk and Fairy Tales*.
Kate follows the "sick" prince to fairyland where he dances every night away. She frees him of the spell and makes her bewitched sister beautiful again.

The Lad in Search of a Fortune
from *Cap o' Rushes*.
A farm lad sets out to find a rich man's daughter and rescue her, but is himself rescued by a wise country lass instead.

The Lass Who Went Out at the Cry of Dawn
from *Thistle and Thyme, Womenfolk and Fairy Tales*.
With her mother's and her father's gifts and blessings and her own bravery, a young woman rescues her sister from an evil enchanter.

The Lion's Whiskers*
A woman tames a lion in order to win the love of her little stepson.

Little Bear
from *With a Wig, With a Wag*.
The youngest of three daughters in this Ojibwa tale is a little bear. She saves her sisters from a powerful old woman, then wins husbands for them and herself by recovering from the woman the sun, the moon, and the north star.

The Little Daughter of the Snow
from *Old Peter's Russian Tales*.
For once it is a daughter, not a son, who is longed for. The girl the old couple make out of snow is active and independent.

Little Hen Eagle
from *Behind the Back of the Mountain*.
Little Hen Eagle fears her brother's pet leopard and kills it. She is sent to her sister to escape her brother's anger, but her servant takes her place. Little Hen Eagle proves her identity by magic.

The Little Horse of Seven Colors*
A Moorish princess helps a captive Christian count to escape. An embrace from his old nurse causes him to forget his princess, but she dresses as a groom and leads her horse to his wedding, breaking the spell. Portuguese.

The Magic Pumpkin*
An old woman tricks a wolf and a tiger, who want to eat her, into fighting each other.

The Man Who Had a Good Wife
from *Yes and No Stories*.
The good wife disguises herself and tricks her lazy husband into becoming industrious.

Mary Culhane and the Dead Man
from *The Goblin's Giggle*.
Mary keeps her wits about her even under the power of a dead man, and wins three pots of gold.

Mighty Wrestlers
from *The World of Nonsense*.
Everyone in this tall tale from India is prodigiously strong: the (male) wrestlers, one wrestler's wife and daughter, an old woman, and the old woman's daughter.

Mr. Fox
from *More English Folk and Fairy Tales, Womenfolk and Fairy Tales*.
Lady Mary investigates the castle of her fiancé and finds him to be a Bluebeard; her brothers and friends destroy him.

Mollie Whuppie
from *English Folk & Fairy Tales, Favorite Fairy Tales Told in England*. Also in *Tales Told Again* and *Womenfolk and Fairy Tales* in a less violent version.
The English girl who steals the giant's treasures and wins three princes as husbands for her sisters and herself.

Molly and the Giant*
"Mollie Whuppie" in an Irish setting.

Mutsmag
from *Grandfather Tales*.
An Appalachian tale similar to "Mollie Whuppie" except that Mutsmag wins gold, not husbands.

The Old Woman and Her Dumpling
from *Japanese Fairy Tales, Womenfolk and Fairy Tales*.
Her rolling dumpling leads her to the land of the wicked Oni but she escapes by making them laugh.

The Old Woman and the Red Pumpkin*
A brief picture-book version of the story in *The Magic Pumpkin*.

The Old Woman Who Lived in a Vinegar Bottle*
The old woman finds she prefers self-sufficiency to the high living a magic fish brings. English.

The Princess and the Magical Hat
from *Mouse Woman and the Vanished Princesses*.
Princess Slender One is stolen away by the stupid son of Great-Whirlpool-Maker, who accidentally leaves behind his father's whirlpool-making hat, enabling Mouse Woman and Slender One's mother to rescue her. A Northwest Coast Indian story.

The Prisoner
from *The Sky-Eater, The Arbuthnot Anthology*.
A huge fish swallows Rangi when she refuses to marry him. She cuts her way out through the thin flesh of his throat, which is why all fish have gills today. Rarotonga.

Queen o' the Tinkers
from *The Well o' the World's End, Hibernian Nights, Princesses and Peasant Boys*.
Fiona refuses to marry the King of Ireland's son, for she has never seen and does not love him. When her angry father forces her to marry, she chooses a handsome tinker who is, of course, the prince in disguise. In "King Thrushbeard," a similar story, the woman is made to seem unreasonable and cruel in refusing to marry and is "taught a lesson."

The Salt at Dinner
from *Rumanian Folk Tales*.
Similar to "Cap o' Rushes."

The Skull
from *The Book of Ghosts and Goblins*.
An orphan girl de-haunts and wins a castle by defending a skull from the skeleton that wants to steal it.

The Slaying of the Sea-Serpent
from *Animal Folk Tales Around the World*.
Tokoyo's father is banished for an affront to the Mikado. She fails to find him, so offers to replace a weeping maiden as the annual sacrifice to the sea-serpent. She kills the serpent, finds near it a long-lost statue of the Mikado, and restores her father to favor.

Spin, Weave, Wear
from *Heather and Broom*.
This starts like Rumpelstiltsken, but the lass pays in advance for the magic, and strikes a better bargain.

The Squire's Bride*
also in *True and Untrue, Norwegian Folk Tales*.
The wealthy old squire won't take "No!" for an answer, so the farmer's daughter makes him look ridiculous.

The Stolen Bairn and the Sidh
from *Thistle and Thyme, Womenfolk and Fairy Tales*.
A woman buys back her stolen child from the fairies by making a cloak and harp without equal in the world.

The Story of Oskus-ool and His Wise Wife

from *How the Moolah Was Taught a Lesson.*
Oskus-ool wins wealth and a wife from the old wolf. The wife's beauty draws the envy of the Khan's son, but her wisdom and knowledge of magic protect her. Tuvin (USSR).

Strega Nona*

The good witch's apprentice uses the forbidden pot and inundates the town with pasta. The townspeople want to string him up, but Strega Nona says "Let the punishment fit the crime" and makes him eat all the pasta.

Tamlane

from *More English Folk and Fairy Tales.* Retold from the ballad.
Burd Janet rescues Tamlane from the fairies by holding him as they change him into one frightening thing after another.

This Time, Tempe Wick?*

A girl outwits the soldiers involved in the 1781 mutiny in Pennslyvania.

Three Sisters Who Were Entrapped into a Mountain

from *Womenfolk and Fairy Tales.*
The troll's youngest captive brings her two sisters back to life, tricks the troll into carrying them home, then escapes herself.

Three Strong Women*

also in *Womenfolk and Fairy Tales.*
The proud wrestler Forever Mountain is trained to be an invincible opponent by a girl, her mother, and her grandmother.

Timo and the Princess Vendla

from *Tales from a Finnish Tupa, Princesses and Peasant Boys.*
The wise Vendla has been taught the languages of every nation, but a shepherd lad fulfills the king's task by knowing the languages of the birds and the beasts, which she does not. He wins Vendla's heart by saying "Vendla is still the most learned lady in the land, for she has admitted ignorance, and truly, the greatest wisdom is to know that one does not know everything."

Turnabout*

A version of "The Husband Who Was to Mind the House" with an updated ending in which the farmer and his wife help each other from time to time.

Twelve Brothers

from *Household Stories from the Collection of the Brothers Grimm, Womenfolk and Fairy Tales.*
A princess remains silent in the face of death in order to free her brothers from an enchantment. Also called "The Six Swans."

The Two Old Women's Bet

from *Grandfather Tales.*
They bet on which one can make a bigger fool out of her own husband. One convinces her spouse he is dead, the other makes hers a suit like "The Emperor's New Clothes."

Umai

from *The Inland Whale.*
A Native American legend in which the lake girl canoes to the ocean and meets the shining girl of the sunset.

Unanana and the Elephant

from *African Myths and Legends, Womenfolk and Fairy Tales.*
Unanana rescues her two children and all the other people who were swallowed alive by the elephant.

The Widow and the Hedley Kow

from *Cap o' Rushes.*
A sensible old woman reforms the local goblin. English.

Wild Robin*

Willful Robin is carried away by the fairies, but his elder sister rescues him. A "Tamlane" for younger children.

Winter Rose

from *Milky Way.*
Two sisters, searching for rose petals to cure their sick mother, fall into the clutches of a wizard, but trick him and escape with the roses.

The Wise Wife

from *Eurasian Folk and Fairy Tales.*
A Russian story similar to, but longer than, "Clever Manka."

The Woman of the Wood*

One man carves a woman from wood, another makes clothes for her, a third teaches her to think and speak. Each claims ownership, but when they ask a wise man to decide, he says she belongs to herself, and must make her own choice. She chooses him.

The Woman Tribe

from *South American Wonder Tales*.
Legend of the warrior women of the Amazon Basin of Brazil.

The Woman Who Flummoxed the Fairies

from *Heather and Broom, Clever Cooks, Womenfolk and Fairy Tales*.
A woman renowned for her light cakes is stolen by the fairies, but tricks them into letting her go.

The Wood Fairy

from *Favorite Fairy Tales Told in Czechoslovakia*.
Retold from "The Wood Maiden."

The Wood Maiden

from *Czechoslovak Fairy Tales*.
A wood fairy entices a young girl to dance and the girl's neglected work is done by magic.

The Young Head of the Family

from *The Fairy Ring*.
A Chinese story of a girl who knows how to carry fire in paper (a lantern) and wind in paper (a fan). Her widowed father-in-law designates her head of the family and she leads it to prosperity.

GODDESSES

The Greek, Roman and Norse mythologies include many well-known stories about goddesses. Here are a few from other cultures.

The Buried Moon

from *More English Fairy Tales*.
The moon rescues a man from the Evil Things in the Carland bog, but is herself captured. With the Wise Woman's guidance, the villagers rescue her.

The Living Kuan-Yin

from *Tales from China*.
The goddess answers three questions for each pilgrim, but the generous Chin Po-wan promises three answers to those he meets along the way. How will his own question be answered?

Song of Sedna*

The legend of an Eskimo woman becoming goddess of the sea.

White Wave, A Chinese Tale*

A moon goddess, in the form of a moon snail, helps a poor, shy farmer.

ANIMAL TALES AND OTHER NON-HUMAN FEMALES

The Cock, the Mouse and the Little Red Hen*

The hen rescues her lazy housemates from the fox.

The Five Little Foxes and the Tiger

from *Animal Folk Tales Around the World*.
Mrs. Fox saves herself and Mr. Fox from the tiger by using her wits, and brings her conceited husband down a peg at the same time. Bangladesh.

The Little Red Hen*

She will not share the product of her work with those who refused to help.

Luck and Wit

from *Rumanian Folk Tales*.
A contest between Luck (masculine) and Wit (feminine) in which Wit wins.

Rabbit and Hedgehog

from *American Negro Folktales*.
Old lady Hedge and her daughter outwit Rabbit in a race.

The Wolf and the Seven Little Kids*

also in the *Arbuthnot Anthology of Children's Literature* and other collections.
The mother goat saves her kids and kills the wolf.

The Wolf Who Had a Wonderful Dream*

A wolf tries to catch and eat a hen, who thwarts him every time.

MODERN FAIRY TALES

The Forest Princess*

The princess rescues the prince from shipwreck, but not from his traditional role.

The Handsome Prince*

from *Just Enough to Make a Story*.
The "sleeping beauty" does not want to be kissed. The prince insists, to his regret.

Petronella*

also in *The Practical Princess and Other Liberating Fairy Tales*.
The third child of a royal couple performs the enchanter's three difficult tasks to rescue a prince, then she has second thoughts about him.

The Practical Princess*
Commonsense Bedelia destroys a dragon, outwits an unwanted suitor, and rescues a prince.

The Silver Whistle*
also in *The Practical Princess and Other Liberating Fairy Tales*.
Prudence, who is plain but has a merry heart and a lively mind, makes her own way in the world with the help of a magic whistle. She turns down the opportunity to become more beautiful by looking into a magic mirror because ". . . I'd be the same inside, and I'm used to me the way I am."

A Story for Heather
from *Just Enough to Make a Story*.
Heather escapes from the crossnore's clutches by whittling and whistling.

ROLE-BREAKING MALES
The Fair Prince and His Brothers
from *Cap o' Rushes*.
The prince who will not fight, wins.

The Laidly Worm of Spindlestone Heugh
from *English Folk and Fairy Tales*.
Childe Wind rescues his sister by kissing the dragon, not by slaying it.

Philbert the Fearful*
also in *The Practical Princess and Other Liberating Fairy Tales*
A knight survives to rescue the emperor's daughter because his lack of machismo keeps him from getting killed on the way. A modern fairy tale.

Princess Heart O'Stone
from *Dream Weaver*.
Donnal takes the burden of the stone heart on his back, and the princess can laugh, cry, and love. A modern fairy tale.

The Woodcutter's Story
from *Plum Pudding*.
The youngest prince gets where he needs to go by letting himself be sidetracked from his princely role. A modern fairy tale.

BOOKS IN WHICH THE STORIES APPEAR

African Myths and Legends. Kathleen Arnott. Walck, 1962, o.p. Unanana and the Elephant.

African Wonder Tales. Frances Carpenter. Doubleday, 1963, o.p. Clever Kadra.

American Negro Folktales. Richard M. Dorson. Fawcett, 1967. Rabbit and Hedgehog.

Animal Folktales Around the World. Kathleen Arnott. Walck, 1971, o.p. The Slaying of the Sea Serpent, The Five Little Foxes and the Tiger.

The Arbuthnot Anthology of Children's Literature. May Hill Arbuthnot. Scott Foresman, 3rd ed. 1971. The Prisoner, The Wolf and the Seven Little Kids.

The Beggar in the Blanket and Other Vietnamese Tales. Gail B. Graham. Dial, 1970. Title story.

Behind the Back of the Mountain, Black Folktales from Southern Africa. Verna Aardema. Dial, 1973. Little Hen Eagle.

The Blue Fairy Book. Andrew Lang. Longmans, Green, ca. 1889, o.p. Dover reprint. The Forty Thieves.

The Book of Ghosts and Goblins. Ruth Manning-Sanders. Dutton, 1973. The Skull.

A Book of Giants. Ruth Manning-Sanders. Dutton, 1963. Fin M'Coul and Cucullin.

Cap o' Rushes and other Folk Tales. Winifred Finlay. Harvey, 1974. Cap o' Rushes, The Black Bull of Norroway, The Fair Prince and His Brothers, The Lad in Search of a Fortune, The Widow and the Hedley Kow.

Chinese Fairy Tales. Isabelle C. Chang. Barre, 1965, o.p. Chinese Red Riding Hoods.

Clever Cooks: A Concoction of Stories, Charms, Recipes and Riddles. Ellin Greene. Lothrop, 1973. Clever Grethel, Clever Oonagh, The Woman Who Flummoxed the Fairies.

The Cock, the Mouse and the Little Red Hen. Felicite Lefevre. Macrae, 1947.

Czechoslovak Fairy Tales. Parker Fillmore. Harcourt, 1919, o.p. The Betrothal Gifts, The Wood Maiden.

Dream Weaver. Jane Yolen. Collins, 1979. Princess Heart O'Stone.

East of the Sun and West of the Moon. P. C. Asbjornsen (several editions). Title story, The Husband Who Was to Mind the House.

English Folk and Fairy Tales. Joseph Jacobs. Putnam, 1904. Dover reprint as *English Fairy Tales.* Cap o' Rushes, Kate Crackernuts, Mollie Whuppie, The Laidly Worm of Spindlestone Heugh.

Eurasian Folk and Fairy Tales. I. F. Bulatkin. Abelard, 1965, o.p. The Wise Wife.

The Fairy Ring. Kate Douglas Wiggin. Doubleday, o.p. The Young Head of the Family.

Favorite Fairy Tales Told in Czechoslovakia. Virginia Haviland. Little, Brown, 1966. The Wood Fairy.

Favorite Fairy Tales Told in England. Virginia Haviland. Little, Brown, 1959. Cap o' Rushes, Mollie Whuppie.

Fools and Funny Fellows. Phyllis Fenner. Knopf, 1947. The Barber's Clever Wife, Clever Manka.

The Forest Princess. Harriet Herman. Over the Rainbow Press, 1974.

Free To Be . . . You And Me. Marlo Thomas. McGraw, 1974. Atalanta.

The Goblin's Giggle and Other Stories. Molly Garret Bang. Scribners, 1973. Mary Culhane and the Dead Man, title story.

Grandfather Tales. Richard Chase. Houghton, 1948. Mutsmag, Two Old Women's Bet.

Half a Kingdom. Ann McGovern. Warne, 1977.

The Handsome Prince. Nancy Schimmel. Franciscan Films, 1975 (film).

Heather and Broom: Tales of the Scottish Highlands. Sorche Nic Leodhas. Holt, 1960. The Gay Goss-hawk; Spin, Weave, Wear; The Woman Who Flummoxed the Fairies.

Hibernian Nights. Seumas MacManus. Macmillan, 1963. Queen o' the Tinkers.

Household Stories from the Collection of the Brothers Grimm. Lucy Crane, translator (several editions). Twelve Brothers (Six Swans), Clever Grethel, The Wolf and the Seven Little Kids.

How the Moolah Was Taught a Lesson and Other Tales from Russia. Estelle Titiev and Lila Pargment. Dial, 1976. The Story of Oskus-ool and His Wise Wife.

The Inland Whale. Theodora Krober. Indiana U. Press, o.p. U. of California Press, 1959. Umai.

Japanese Fairy Tales. Lafcadio Hearn. Peter Pauper, 1948. The Old Woman and Her Dumpling.

Just Enough to Make a Story. Nancy Schimmel. Sisters' Choice, 1978. The Handsome Prince, A Story for Heather.

The Lion's Whiskers, Tales of High Africa. Brent Ashabranner and Russell Davis. Little, Brown, 1959. Title story.

The Little Red Hen. Janina Domanska. Macmillan, 1973. Paul Galdone. Seabury, 1973. English/Spanish edition, Letty Williams. Prentice, 1969.

The Little Horse of Seven Colors and Other Portuguese Folk Tales. Patricia Lowe. World, 1970, o.p.

Magic Animals of Japan. Davis Pratt. Parnassus, 1967. The Dragon's Revenge, A Fox Who Was Too Sly.

The Magic Orange Tree and Other Haitian Folktales. Diane Wolkstein. Knopf, 1978. I'm Tipingee, She's Tipingee, We're Tipingee, Too.

The Man in the Moon: Sky Tales from Many Lands. Alta Jablow and Carl Withers. Holt, 1969, o.p. The Girl Who Overpowered the Moon.

The Milky Way and Other Chinese Folk Tales. Adet Lin. Harcourt, 1961. Winter Rose.

Molly and the Giant. Kurt Werth and Mabel Watts. Parents, 1973.

The Moon Painters and Other Estonian Folktales. Selve Mass. Viking, 1971. The Clever Peasant Girl.

More English Folk and Fairy Tales. Joseph Jacobs. Putnam, 1904. Dover reprint as *More English Fairy Tales.* The Black Bull of Norroway, Mr. Fox, Tamlane.

Mouse Woman and the Vanished Princesses. Christie Harris. Atheneum, 1976. The Princess and the Magical Hat.

Norwegian Folk Tales. Peter Asbjornsen. Viking, 1960. The Squire's Bride.

Old Peter's Russian Tales. Arthur Ransome. Nelson, 1916, o.p. Dover reprint. Little Daughter of the Snow, Baba Yaga.

The Old Woman Who Lived in a Vinegar Bottle. Rumer Godden. Viking, 1970. Penguin, 1974.

People of the Short Blue Corn: Tales and Legends of the Hopi Indians. Harold Courlander. Harcourt, 1970. The Foot Racers of Payupki.

Petronella. Jay Williams. Parents, 1973.

Philbert the Fearful. by Jay Williams. Norton, 1966.

Plum Pudding: Stories and Songs with Nancy Schimmel and the Plum City Players. Sisters' Choice Records, 1982. The Woodcutter's Story.

The Practical Princess. Jay Williams. Parents, 1969.

The Practical Princess and Other Liberating Fairy Tales. Jay Williams. Four Winds, 1978, Scholastic. Petronella, The Practical Princess, Philbert the Fearful.

Princesses and Peasant Boys: Tales of Enchantment. Phyllis Fenner. Knopf, 1944, o.p. Timo and the Princess Vendla, Queen o' the Tinkers.

Rumanian Folk Tales. Jean Ure. Watts, 1960, o.p. Luck and Wit, The Salt at Dinner.

Russian Wonder Tales. Post Wheeler. Thomas Yoseloff, 1957, o.p. The Feather of Finist the Falcon.

Scandinavian Stories. Margaret Sperry. Watts, 1971, o.p. The Golden Shoe.

The Shepherd's Nosegay, Stories from Finland and Czechoslovakia. Parker Fillmore. Harcourt, 1920, o.p. Clever Manka.

The Silver Whistle. Jay Williams. Parents, 1971.

The Sky-Eater and Other South Sea Tales. James Holding. Abelard, 1965, o.p. The Prisoner.

Song of Sedna. Robert San Souci. Doubleday, 1981.

South American Wonder Tales. Frances Carpenter. Follett, 1969. Clever Carmelita, The Woman Tribe.

The Squire's Bride. P. C. Asbjornsen, illus. Marcia Sewall. Atheneum, 1975.

Strega Nona; An Old Tale. Tomie De Paola. Prentice-Hall, 1975.

Tales from a Finnish Tupa. James Bowman and Margery Bianco. Albert Whitman, 1936. Timo and the Princess Vendla.

Tales from China. Carol Kendall and Yao-wen Li. Seabury, 1979. The Living Kuan-Yin.

Tales from the Punjab. Flora A. Steele. Macmillan, 1894, o.p. The Barber's Clever Wife.

Tales Told Again. Walter de la Mare. Knopf, 1927. Clever Grethel, Mollie Whuppie.

This Time, Tempe Wick? Patricia Gauch. Coward, 1974.

Thistle and Thyme, Tales and Legends from Scotland. Sorche Nic Leodhas. Holt, 1962, o.p. The Lass Who Went Out at the Cry of Dawn, The Stolen Bairn and the Sidh.

Three Strong Women: A Tall Tale from Japan. Claus Stamm. Viking, 1962.

Time for Fairy Tales, Old and New. May Hill Arbuthnot. Scott, 1961. Clever Manka, The Husband Who Was to Mind the House.

True and Untrue, and Other Norse Tales. Sigrid Undset. Knopf, 1945, o.p. The Squire's Bride, The Husband Who Was to Mind the House, East of the Sun and West of the Moon.

Turnabout: A Norwegian Tale. William Wiesner. Seabury, 1972.

The Well o' the World's End. Seumas MacManus. Macmillan, 1939, o.p. Queen o' the Tinkers.

White Wave, a Chinese Tale. Diane Wolkstein. T. Y. Crowell, 1979.

Wild Robin. Susan Jeffers. Dutton, 1976.

William Mayne's Book of Giants. Dutton, 1969. Clever Oonagh.

With a Wig, With a Wag, and Other American Folk Tales. Jean Cothran. David McKay, 1954, o.p. Little Bear.

The Wolf and the Seven Little Kids. The Brothers Grimm. Harcourt, o.p.

The Wolf Who Had a Wonderful Dream: A French Tale. Anne Rockwell, T. Y. Crowell, 1973.

The Woman of the Wood: A Tale from Old Russia. Algernon D. Black. Holt, 1973.

Womenfolk and Fairy Tales. Rosemary Minard. Houghton, 1975. The Stolen Bairn and the Sidh, The Chinese Red Riding Hoods, Molly Whuppie, Mr. Fox, The Twelve Brothers, The Old Woman and Her Dumpling, The Forty Thieves, Kate Crackernuts, Clever Grethel, Cap o' Rushes, The Lass Who Went Out at the Cry of Dawn, Three Strong Women, The Husband Who Was to Mind the House, East of the Sun and West of the Moon, Unanana and the Elephant, the Woman Who Flummoxed the Fairies, Clever Manka, The Three Sisters Who Were Entrapped into a Mountain.

The World of Nonsense, Strange and Humorous Tales from Many Lands. Carl Withers, Holt, 1968, o.p. Mighty Wrestlers.

The World's Great Stories: 55 Legends That Live Forever. Louis Untermeyer. Evans/Lippincott, 1964. Boadicea . . . the Warrior Queen.

Yes and No Stories. George and Helen Papashivley. Harper, 1946, o.p. Davit, The Man Who Had a Good Wife.

This list was revised and annotated by Nancy Schimmel, but many others have contributed information: Camille Pronger, Marion Callery Morter, Dolly Larvick Barnes, Kendall Smith, Northern California Association of Children's Librarians—Social Concerns Committee, ALA-ALSC Discussion Group on Sexism in Library Materials for Children, University of Wisconsin Library School Storytelling Class, Summer 1977 and 1981.

Another source is *Stories: A List of Stories to Tell and to Read Aloud*, New York Public Library, 7th edition, 1977, which lists 45 stories of "Clever and Heroic Women," mostly folktales, on page 76.

Active Heroines in Folktales for Children may be reproduced in its entirety only, including introduction and credits, by any library, school, or other non-profit organization, without permission.

Sisters' Choices

HERE ARE SOME STORIES WE HAVE TOLD, with sources, additional comments, and *approximate* age range.

The Basket
from *Patterns of Renewal*, by Laurens Van der Post. Pendle Hill Pamphlet number 121, 1962. Pendle Hill Publications, Wallingford, PA 19086.
A short commentary on marriage, among other things. 12–adult.

The Bear Says North
from *The Shepherd's Nosegay*, by Parker Fillmore. Harcourt, 1920, o.p.
A good short one . . . but your listeners have to be watchers too. Finnish. 6–12.

The Boy Who Had No Story to Tell
from *Folktales of the Irish Countryside*, by Kevin Danaher. D. White, 1970.
A ghost story on the uses of storytelling. 10–adult.

Caps for Sale
by Esphyr Slobodkina. Addison-Wesley, 1947, Scholastic pbk. 1976.
Russian. 3–6.

The Cat on the Dovrefell
from *East of the Sun and West of the Moon*, by P. C. Asbjornsen, trans. George Dasent. Dover, 1970.
An unsentimental Christmas story, from Norway, with trolls. 6–11.

Clever Manka
from *The Shepherd's Nosegay*.
A riddle story. Czechoslovakian. 10–adult.

Did the Tailor Have a Nightmare?
from *Let's Steal the Moon: Jewish Tales, Ancient and Recent*, by Blanch Serwer. Little, 1970.
An encounter with Napoleon. 11–adult.

Equinoctial and Phoebe
from *Folk Songs of Peggy Seeger*. Oak, 1964.
A ballad. United States. 6–adult.

The Fat Cat, a Danish Folktale
by Jack Kent. Parents, 1971, Scholastic pbk. 1972.
As a dramatized story, best with mixed ages, 3–6 to 3–adult. As a picture book, 4–7.

Fiddler, Play Fast, Play Faster
from *The Long Christmas*, by Ruth Sawyer. Viking, 1941.
A fairly shivery Christmas story from the Isle of Man. 11–adult.

The Foolish Frog
by Pete Seeger and Charles Seeger. Macmillan, c. 1955.
I introduce this *cante fable* by saying it's a story about the olden times when most daddies didn't know how to cook supper. Good for mixed-age audiences, all children or children and adults.

The Handsome Prince
This story is also available as a seven-minute 16mm color film from Franciscan Films, P.O. Box 6116, San Francisco, CA 94101, for rent or sale.

The Huckabuck Family and How They Raised Pop Corn in Nebraska and Quit and Came Back
from *Rootabaga Stories*, by Carl Sandburg. Harcourt, 1922.
A Thanksgiving story that isn't thankful. 6–9.

I'm Tipingee, She's Tipingee, We're Tipingee Too
from *The Magic Orange Tree and Other Haitian Folktales*, by Diane Wolkstein. Knopf, 1978.
I tell this as I saw Diane tell it, asking individual girls to wear red to help Tipingee trick the old man. Since this is yet another bad stepmother story, I generally follow it with "The Lion's Whisker." Good for mixed-age audiences.

It Could Always Be Worse

by Margot Zemach. Farrar, Straus, 1977.
My mother used to tell me this one, so I don't follow the book closely, but I do keep it kosher—no pigs. It's fun to do as an audience participation story with groups of children being the family and animals. All ages.

The Journey

from *Mouse Tales* by Arnold Lobel. Harper, 1972.
The mouse gets a new pair of feet. 4–7.

The King o' the Cats

from *More English Fairy Tales*.
I introduce this by saying "This is a story from the old times when the graveyard was right next to the church, so the sexton, who takes care of the church, also dug the graves." That takes care of "sexton" without sounding quite like a definition. 7–adult.

Kiss Me

from *Rootabaga Stories*.
An adventure for Valentine's Day or any time. 6–11, adult.

The Laidly Worm of Spindlestone Heugh

from *English Fairy Tales*, by Joseph Jacobs. Dover pbk.
Jacobs retold this from a ballad whose tune has been lost. I found that the tune of "The Cottage Door" in *Folk Songs of Peggy Seeger* fits the meter and mood of Lady Margaret's verses in this story exactly, so I sing them to that tune. 10–adult.

Lazy Jack

from *English Fairy Tales*.
I don't like the idea of the girl's father handing her over to Jack as a reward, so I have Jack court her first. Gives her time to grow up, too—"girls" are too young to get married. 4–10.

The Lion on the Path

by Hugh Tracey. Routledge and Kegan Paul, London, 1967.
A farmer entrances a threatening lion with his thumb piano, but is stuck until Rabbit helps him escape. I tell this with a thumb piano. 5–adult.

The Lion-Makers

from *Once Upon a Time* by Rose Dobbs. Random, 1950.
This is a translation by Arthur Ryder from the *Panchatantra*, a collection used for the education of princes in India, circa 500 A.D. It is as current as today's headlines, being a commentary on the arrogance of experts. Another version is "The Scholars and the Lion" in Courlander's *The Tiger's Whisker*. 7–adult.

The Lion's Whiskers

from *The Lion's Whiskers, Tales of High Africa* by Brent Ashabranner and Russell Davis. Little, Brown, 1959.
The only story I've found with a good stepmother—and a hint of why there are so many stories with bad ones. 7–adult.

The Little Red Hen

I learned this story from my mother. There are many versions—the one I tell doesn't say anything about the hen sharing the bread with her chicks. English. 4–6.

Magic Wings

by Dianne Wolkstein. Little, Brown (forthcoming, 1983).
This version of an old Chinese tale (found as "Growing Wings" in Adet Lin's *The Milky Way*) is the one I prefer to tell, as Diane's goose girl is not wimpy. I tell it as Diane does, getting four children up front flapping their arms, and flying the goose girl at the end (see photo on back cover). Pre-school–adult.

The Man Who Walked on Water

from *Tales of the Dervishes* by Idris Shah. Dutton, 1970.
After one of my students told this story about how it's okay to make mistakes, she immediately said, "I made a mistake—I forgot to say that reciting the text would bring you to such a high state of enlightenment *that you could walk on water*." The class reaction was that the story was much better her way—just knowing that the text can produce a high state of enlightenment, but not knowing about walking on water till the very end. So it really *is* okay to make mistakes. (However, I think it would be a mistake to announce the title of the story before you told it). Adult.

Mr. Fox

from *English Fairy Tales*.
The English Bluebeard. 11–adult.

The Mujina

from *Tales to Be Told in the Dark*, by Basil Davenport. Dodd, 1953. "Two Anecdotes," p. 245.
A Japanese ghost story retold by Lafcadio Hearn. 12–adult.

The Musician of Tagaung

from *The Tiger's Whisker, and Other Tales of the Asia and the Pacific*, by Harold Courlander. Harcourt, 1959.
I like to tell this Burmese tale at folk music gatherings. The book has other good stories to tell to adults. 10–adult.

The Old Woman and Her Pig

by Paul Galdone. McGraw, 1961.
Remember to start fairly slowly if you want to speed up on the return trip. English. Pre-school.

The Pancake

from *Tales of Laughter,* by Kate Douglas Wiggin. Doubleday, o.p. Also in other collections.
Similar to "The Gingerbread Boy" and "The Bun." Norwegian. Pre-school. As a tandem story, pre-school–8.

Patches

from *Men from the Village Deep in the Mountains,* by Garrett Bang. Macmillan, 1973.
A Japanese tale with a most satisfying ending. 8–adult. When I tell "Patches," I first sing "Sho-joji," also from Japan and also about badgers. It's on *Berman/Barlin: Dance-a-Story, Sing-a-Song,* from Children's Book & Music Center, 2500 Santa Monica Blvd., Santa Monica, CA 90404.

The Pedlar of Swaffham

from *More English Fairy Tales,* by Joseph Jacobs. Dover pbk.
A peddler heeds the message in his dream and finds a treasure. There's a Jewish version in *Souls on Fire: Portraits and Legends of the Hasidic Masters* (o.p.) by Elie Wiesel.

A Penny A Look, An Old Story Retold

by Harve Zemach. Farrar, 1971.
Harve Zemach took an old Japanese tale of a schemer caught in his own scheme and made it the story of a rascal and his lazy brother, in a European setting. The Folktellers changed the brothers to sisters and moved them to the American South, which is the way Gay Ducey tells it, and I'm picking it up from her. The Folktellers do it as a tandem story. 7–adult.

Petronella

by Jay Williams. Parents, 1973. Also in his *The Practical Princess and Other Liberating Fairy Tales.* Four Winds, 1978, Scholastic.
The cleverest twist on the fairy tale theme that I know of. 9–adult.

Señor Coyote and the Dogs

from *Ride with the Sun,* by Harold Courlander. McGraw, 1955.
This story has all the action of a Saturday morning cartoon, and it says something, too. 6–adult.

The Song of Gimmile.

from *The King's Drum and Other African Stories,* by Harold Courlander. Harcourt, 1962.
An arrogant king is forced by ridicule to be just. *One Potato, Two Potato* has a good discussion (p. 161) of folklore as a medium for expressing hostility when it would be unsafe or hurtful to express it directly. This can be incorporated into the introduction to this story or discussed afterward. 8–adult.

The Skull

from *The Book of Ghosts and Goblins,* by Ruth Manning-Sanders. Dutton, 1973.
I prefer to leave the little girl with the castle, servants and playmates she has won away from the skeleton. She doesn't need—and the story doesn't need—the promise of a prince later. Tyrolian. 8–11.

The Three Billy Goats Gruff

by P. C. Asbjornsen, illus. Marcia Brown. Harcourt, 1957, pbk. 1972. Also in *East o' the Sun and West o' the Moon.* Norwegian. 3–7.

Ticoumba and the President

from *The Piece of Fire and Other Haitian Tales,* by Harold Courlander. Harcourt, 1964.
This trickster tale has some of the same riddles used in "Clever Manka" but has an entirely different mood. A good story for two tellers. 10–13.

Umai

from *The Inland Whale,* by Theodora Kroeber. University of California Press, 1959.
A Yurok story from northern Califronia. 10–adult.

Wait Till Martin Comes

from *Tales to Be Told in the Dark,* by Basil Davenport. Dodd, 1953. "Two Anecdotes," p. 245.
A ghost-story spoof, good for telling after a scary one. United States. 8–11.

Where the Wild Things Are

by Maurice Sendak. Harper, 1963.
I would never have had the chuzpah to do Sendak without the illustrations if I hadn't seen the Folktellers do it. They have the audience put on their wolf suits first, and practice roaring their terrible roars, showing their terrible claws, etc. The audience warms up during the description of all the wild things in the story, and lets loose for the wild rumpus—thus taking care of all those pages without text. Pre-school–7.

Who Can Break a Bad Habit?

from *African Wonder Tales,* by Frances Carpenter.
Doubleday, o.p.
This story amuses young children and comments on
the use of gesture in storytelling. 5–9 and adult.

The Wild Ducks and the Goose

by Carl Withers. Holt, 1968.
Chalkboard story. United States, 8–10.

The Wood Maiden

I tell a version I put together from Parker Fillmore's
telling in *Czechoslovakian Fairy Tales* (Harcourt, 1919,
o.p.) and Virginia Haviland's shortened retelling in
Favorite Fairy Tales Told in Czechoslovakia (Little, 1966).
8–10.

The Yam Thief

from *Strings on Your Fingers: How to Make String Figures* by
Harry and Elizabeth Helfman. Morrow, 1965.
From the islands of the Torres Strait. All ages.

Names of Quilt Squares

TITLE INDEX

SUBJECT INDEX